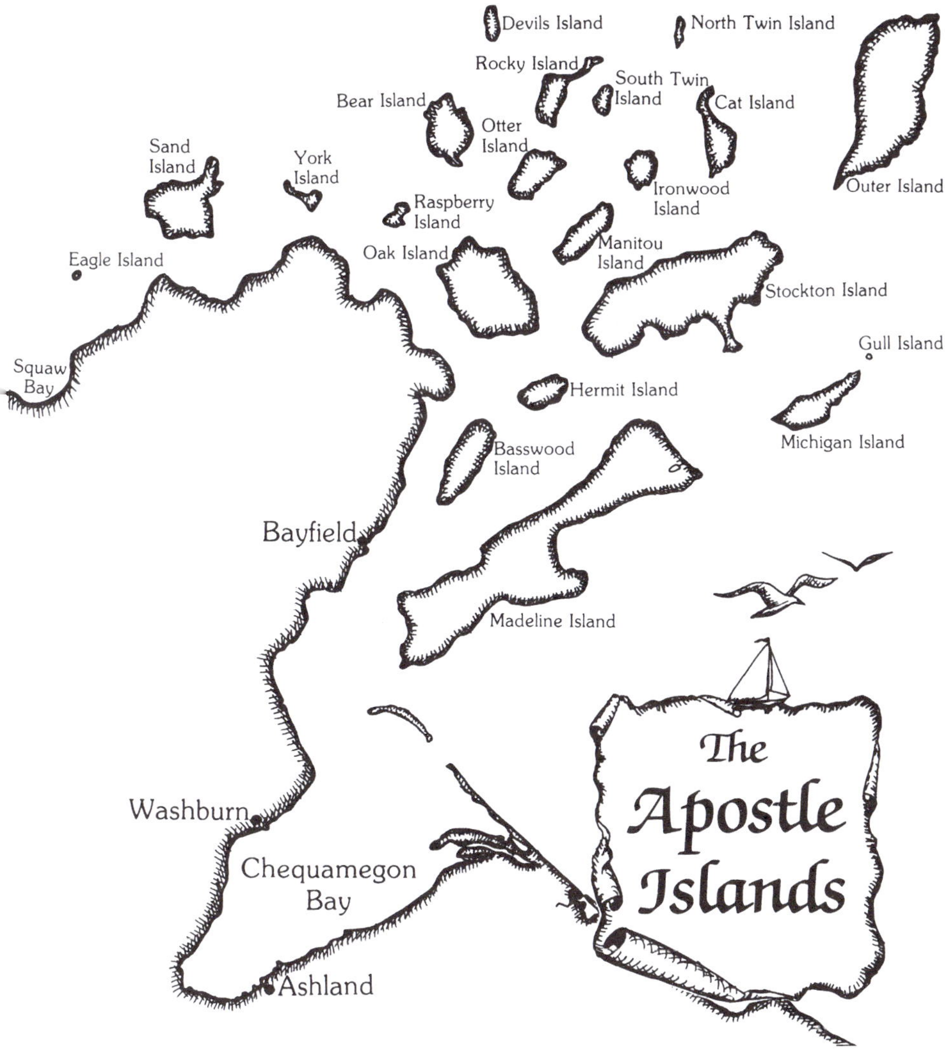
Devils Island
North Twin Island
Rocky Island
South Twin Island
Cat Island
Bear Island
Otter Island
Sand Island
York Island
Outer Island
Raspberry Island
Ironwood Island
Eagle Island
Oak Island
Manitou Island
Stockton Island
Squaw Bay
Gull Island
Hermit Island
Basswood Island
Michigan Island
Bayfield
Madeline Island
Washburn
Chequamegon Bay
Ashland
The Apostle Islands

The Visitor's Guide
to the

APOSTLE ISLANDS NATIONAL LAKESHORE

by
DAVE STRZOK

ISBN 0-9728168-1-X

Previous Printings
July 1981
July 1988
1992
1999

©*copyright 2003*
by Dave Strzok
P.O. Box 691
Bayfield, WI 54814
All Rights Reserved

Table of Contents

I. **About the Visitor's Guide to Apostle Islands National Lakeshore** 1
II. **Guidelines to the Use of the Apostle Islands National Lakeshore** 3
III. **The Apostle Islands**
   Basswood Island 4
   Bear Island 8
   Cat Island 10
   Devils Island 14
   Eagle Island 20
   Gull Island 24
   Hermit Island 28
   Ironwood Island 34
   Long Island 37
   Manitou Island 40
   Michigan Island 44
   North Twin Island 50
   Oak Island 52
   Otter Island 58
   Outer Island 62
   Raspberry Island 70
   Rocky Island 74
   Sand Island 78
   Stockton Island 84
   South Twin Island 94
   York Island 96
   Little Sand Bay 100
   Squaw Bay Caves 104
IV. **Boating Among the Islands** 106
   Float Plan 110
   What to do About the Weather 110
   A Few Observations About Anchoring 114

	Docks and Anchorages 117
	Marine Facilities 118
	About Beaching a Boat on an Island 120
V.	**Marine Radio Communications** 122
VI.	**Fishing Among the Apostle Islands** 126
	When to Fish the Lakes 126
	How to Fish the Lakes 129
VII.	**Camping in the Apostle Islands National Lakeshore** 133
	Getting to the Islands 134
VIII.	**Hiking in the Apostle Islands National Lakeshore** 135
	Fauna and Flora 135
	Swimming 137
	Visitor Services 138
IX	**Essential Cruising and Sailing Information** 139
	Helpful Charts, Reading and Addresses 139
X.	**Updates and National Park Service Reprints** 140
	Apostle Islands National Lakeshore Camping Policy 141
	Welcome Scuba Divers 142
	Island Maps 144-149
	Paddling in the Apostles 155
	Boater's Guide 158
	Stockton Island 160
	Oak Island 164
	Sand Island 169
	Basswood Island 171
	Sea Caves 176

I.

About the Visitor's Guide to the Apostle Islands National Lakeshore

This guide was written primarily for the visitor who is on an island camping or aboard the excursion boats, private powerboats or sailboats. It has often occurred to me, as I boated among the islands, that unless the visitor researched the history books, listened to stories told by the "old timers," looked around on the islands, listened to the excursion boat narrations, skirted along shorelines and spent time feeling the weather and watching the seasons, he would merely enjoy the exhilarating beauty and the expansive majesty of the Lake and the Apostle Islands. So what more might one need than that kind of refreshment? I still wanted to know what other people did who were drawn to these islands, who spent days or lifetimes changing the face of this special part of the earth.

Early Native Americans made legends about the origin of these islands. Their "Original Man" formed the islands from clods of earth he threw at a fleeing buck. Early Native Americans hunted, camped and resided on these islands for a duration of at least 3000 years, judging from archeological discoveries.

At about the time Columbus sailed for North America, Chippewa (Ojibwe) Indians were migrating from the St. Lawrence River Valley region to the shores of Gitchee-Gummee – The Big Sea Water – Lake Superior. They were being led to this new home by a guide – a legendary squirrel named Ojidaumo. The legend is spun out in Longfellow's "Song of Hiawatha."

The Chippewa named the islands after natural or supernatural occurrences – for the oak, the bear, the sand, the rocky beaches, the spirit they experienced. When French missionaries arrived during the 1600's, they named the island group in honor of the twelve apostles. In the 1700's, a mineral surveyor, Henry Schoolcraft, renamed the islands the Federation Islands after the existing states at that time. His names were not widely accepted by local people and the names reverted back to a combination of current local names and Chippewa names. The names, changed and adapted over the years, are an interesting study in history.

Settlement by White men is mostly a story of exploitation of the resources: the cutting of big timber, the sandstone quarrying, trapping of the fur bearing animals, and the fishing. A few stands of virgin timber remind us of the grandeur of the wilderness islands. Quarries can still be seen on the islands. Wildlife has lived through cycles of prosperity and scarcity. The large fish succumbed to the sea lamprey and the fisherman, currently to be restocked by fish management agencies. The islands have regained their near-wilderness condition and will be protected by the National Park Service in the future.

This book is not intended to be an exhaustive document of all the history nor all the facts about the islands. Madeline is not included because it is not part of the National Lakeshore. The story of Madeline Island is well told in several publications. The details concerning the shoals, submerged hazards included in sections on each island are not intended to be all there is to look out for while cruising. There are hundreds of miles of lakeshore among the islands and no assumption should be made that they are all detailed in this book. But what is included in the book will be helpful. The information was gleaned from my twenty-six years of operating a water taxi and excursion boats to the islands.

Finally, the book is intended to give depth to your experience of the islands.

Dave Strzok

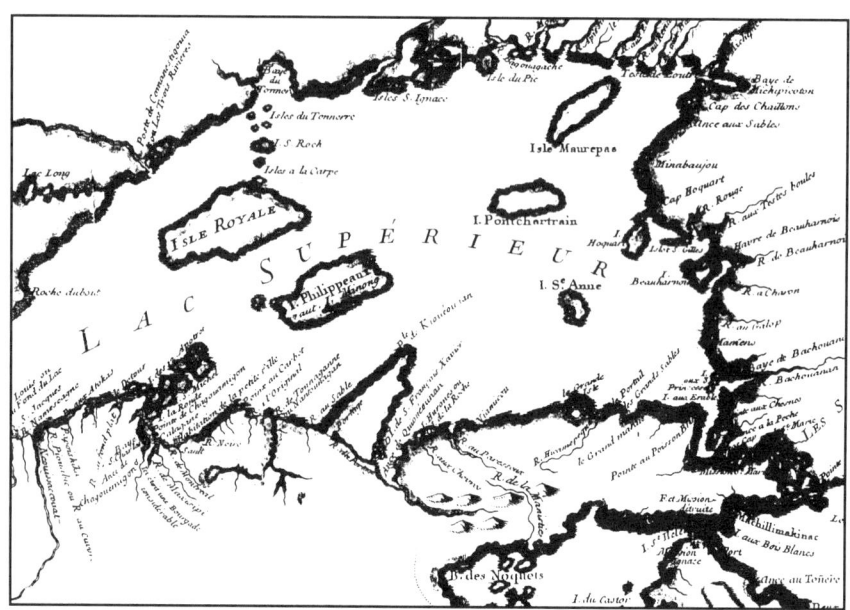

Par N.BELLIN Ingenieur et Hydrographic de la Marine 1744.

II.

Guidelines to the use of the Apostle Islands National Lakeshore

In 1970, 20 of the 22 Apostle Islands and a portion of the mainland off the Bayfield peninsula were designated as a National Lakeshore, a recreational area of 42,000 acres spread out over 600 square miles of Lake Superior. Public Law 91-424 states the purpose of the National Lakeshore is "to conserve and develop for the benefit, inspiration, education, recreational use and enjoyment of the public..." The National Park Service is charged with this duty and carries it out in a number of ways.

Headquarters for the National Lakeshore is situated in the old Bayfield County Courthouse. The Park Service moved into the Courthouse in 1979, after the building had been renovated through the efforts of local people who wished to see the historic old building put to use.

Located on the first floor is the interpretive division of the Park Service. Multiple uses of the Park, guidance and information, displays and presentations are planned and scheduled with the Naturalists. Personnel in this department put on evening campfire programs, present special lectures on history apropos to the Apostle Islands area, lead hikes and walks to outdoor sites, and generally inform visitors about the Apostle Islands.

The Ranger division of the Park Service is primarily concerned with assisting visitors in use and protection of the resources within the Park and the protection of the visitors.

The Administrative department directs the operation of the organization under the supervision of the Superintendent of the Park.

The Maintenance department, as its name indicates, maintains, builds and renovates Park properties.

Personnel from each department will be found throughout the National Lakeshore, performing their tasks primarily during the busy summer months, though winter planning and work is also carried on.

The many uses of the National Lakeshore require decisions based on a number of viewpoints. Proposed use of the many resources within the Park are presented from the points of view of the visitors, protectors, interpreters, environmentalists, historians and researchers. As knowledge of the lake and islands expands, decisions must be made with the best information available. The intent of these many efforts is "to conserve, and develop for the benefit, inspiration, education, recreational use and enjoyment of the public..."

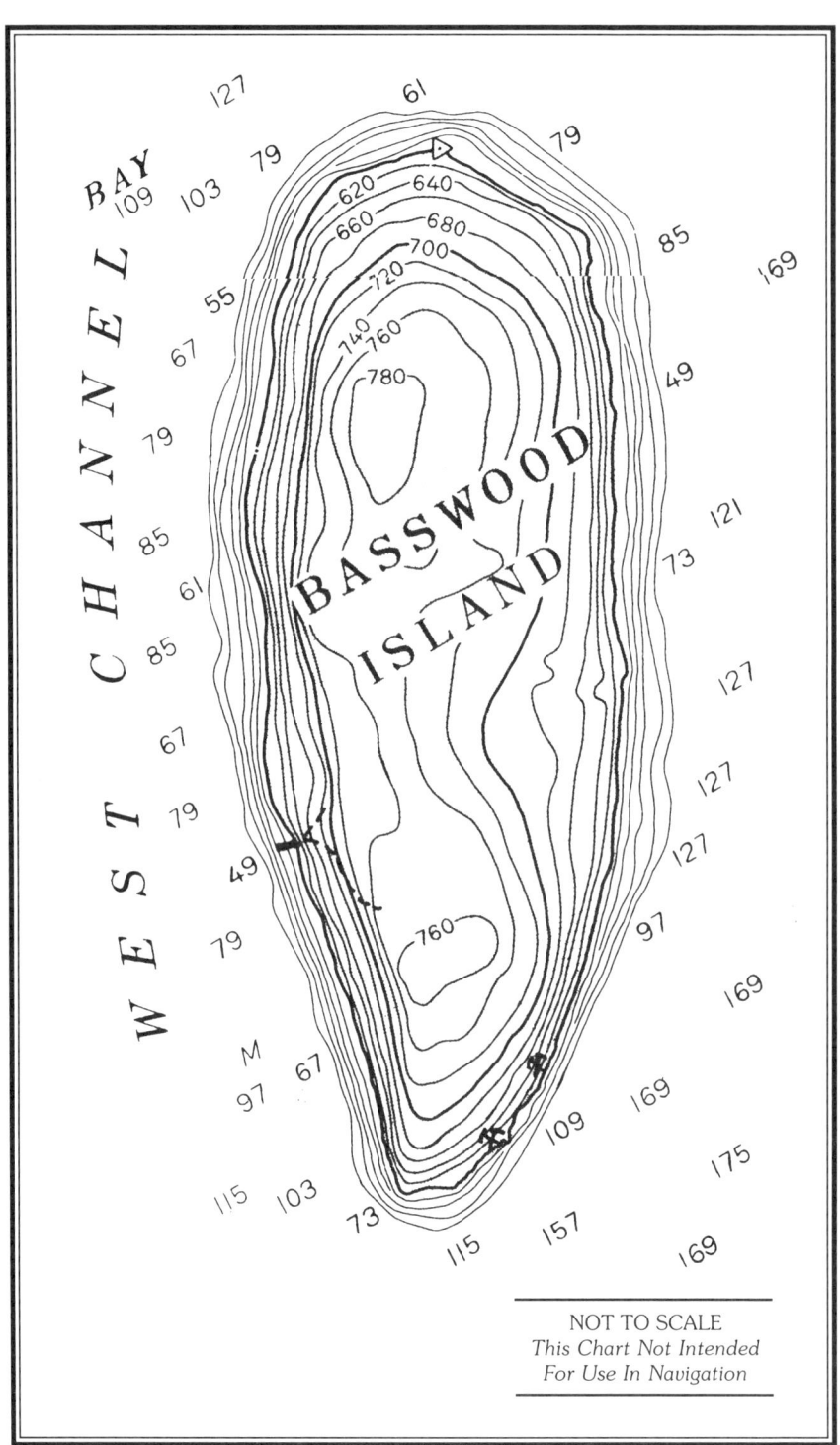

4

III.
Basswood Island

Former Names:
Chippewa name – wigobic miniss (Basswood Island). Schoolcraft's name – Illinois. French name – Michel. Local name – Bass.

Size:
1917 acres, about $3\frac{1}{2}$ miles long, $1\frac{1}{2}$ miles wide.

Characteristics of the Island:
Basswood Island is an oval-shaped, rounded mass with steep, rocky shores, forested primarily with hardwoods about 50 years old. Rugged sandstone ledges and shelves on the south end of the island drop off to deep water. Midway up the length of the island, on the west side, a very small beach has formed at the end of drainage gully. Off the northeast shore of the island, a picturesque standing rock called "Honeymoon Rock," is usually shared by a couple of weather-beaten pines, a few resting seagulls and swallows.

A section of the Superior Brownstone Quarries at Bass Island.
NPS Photo

Historic Sites:

The first of five island sandstone quarries was opened at the south end of Basswood Island in 1868, by Basswood Quarry Co. Materials from this quarry were used in the construction of the Milwaukee Courthouse, as well as the St. Paul Dispatch Building, the St. Paul Globe Building, the St. Paul's Church and the Plankinton Building in Milwaukee, and the Chicago Tribune office. Stories circulate that the Basswood quarry materials were used to rebuild civic buildings in Chicago after the Great Chicago Fire and that some brownstone from the islands was even used in the construction of the Brownstone apartments on Chicago's Lakeshore Drive The Basswood quarry is on the National Register of Historic Places.

Three former farmsites are located in clearings on the island. One is about a mile northeast of the west dock. A few neglected apple trees near a clearing mark the old orchard belonging to this farmstead. Another farmsite is marked by a clearing about 700 yards north of the dock. The third old farmsite lies at the end of a well-marked trail leading southeast from the west dock. A dairy farmer operated a farm here, hauling his butter, cheese and milk by boat from his farmstead to customers across the channel to the village of Red Cliff. He and his family left the island in the 1940's. The clearing was later used in the most recent logging of the island. The island's forests have been harvested at least three times.

Some survey maps, drawn up at a time when residential housing was proposed on the island show streets and lots lining the length of Basswood Island.

Before being incorporated into the National Lakeshore, much of Basswood Island was part of Apostle Islands State Forest.

Moorage and Docking:

Midway up the west side of Basswood Island lies a 70-foot long wooden National Park Service dock. Under normal conditions, a 4 to 5 foot water depth can be found at the outside end of the dock, shallowing gradually up to the beach. About 50 feet of each side of the dock is usable for boats of shallow draft.

Under most wind conditions, the dock is secure from harmful seas. A sand bottom in the vicinity offers good anchorage. Occasional large boats using the west channel send out dangerous wakes for small vessels tied to this dock.

Waters Surrounding the Island:

Between Basswood and the mainland is a deep channel and some of the most protected waters among the islands.

Besides checking the chart for depths, boaters should be aware of the sunken remains of a dock about 5 feet underwater off the main quarry site at the south end of the island.

Fisheries:

A trolling fishery exists along the west shore of Basswood Island to Frog Bay, for brown trout and salmon from spring to early summer and again in October.

Camping:

At the present time, there are special facilities for campers on Basswood Island's clearings. The dairy farm clearing is located about 200 yards southeast of the dock along a well-maintained trail. Two other clearings, one north and the other northeast (the orchard site) of the dock offer potential camping possibilities. The rock ledges at the south end of the island are the most scenic campsites on the island.

Trails:

A few logging trails transect the island (see maps). A groomed trail leads from the dock to the dairy farm clearing. Development of more trails took place in the 1980's and are shown on the Park brochure for Basswood Island

The Vicinity:

Two and a half miles north of Basswood Island lies Oak Island, the tallest of the Apostle Islands. To the northeast lies Hermit Island, a small island with a large history. South and southeast lie the North Channel and Madeline Island, the island stretching about 15 miles from end to end. The West Channel, a mile wide, separates Basswood from the mainland. On the mainland, $2\frac{1}{2}$ miles to the southwest, is Bayfield. To the west lies the Red Cliff Indian Reservation, the Buffalo Bay Marina, the village of Red Cliff, Roys Point Marina and a campground at Red Cliff. Northwest of Basswood is Red Cliff Bay or Schooner Bay.

Honeymoon Rock off the north point of Basswood Island.

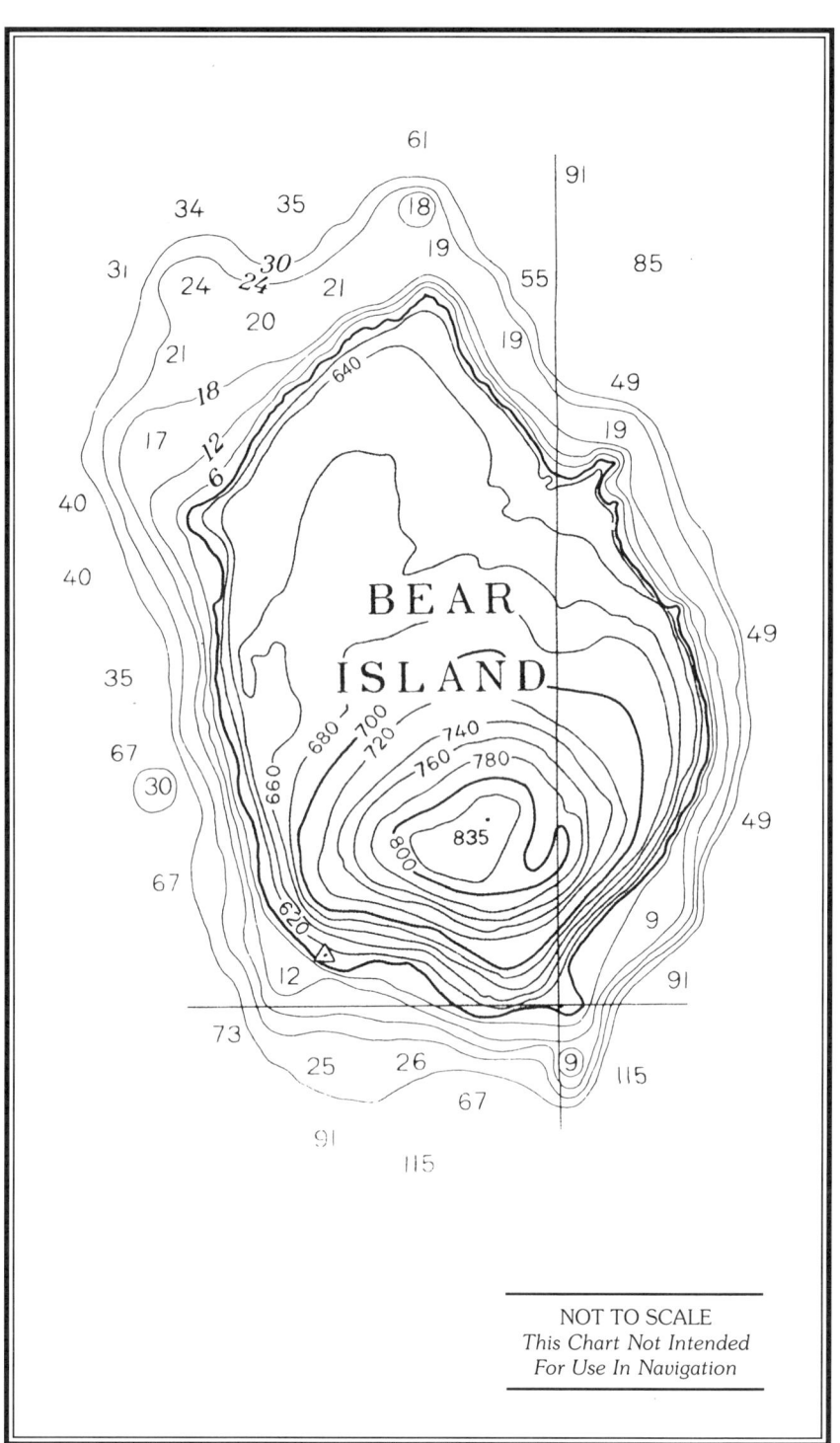

NOT TO SCALE
This Chart Not Intended For Use In Navigation

8

Bear Island

Former Names:
Chippewa – mako miniss (Bear Island).

Size:
1,824 acres.

Characteristics of the Island:
Bear Island is the second tallest island rising nearly 250 feet above the lake level. It is highly forested. An old beach line can be found near the top of the island, evidence of a time when the lake level was more than 200 feet above its present level, and of a time when Bear and Oak Islands were the only islands above the water. The rocky formations at the north end of the island take their shapes from the battering of waves from the northerly quarter. A sandy cove rests between rocky ledges at the northeast corner of the island. Rocky cliffs run the length of the east shore, ending in a sand point at the south end. The west shore of the island is made up of clay cliffs up to the northernmost part of the island where the rocky ledges face the open lake.

In spite of its name, bear are not notorious residents of the island.

Historic Information:
A logging camp was located in the northeast cove, and a fish camp was located at the sand point at the south end of the island.

By virtue of its height, Bear Island was the second island exposed above water as the lake level receded thousands of years ago.

Moorage and Docking:
The sandy bottom east of the south sand point permits an anchorage. An anchorage can also be found in the northeast cove under appropriate wind and wave conditions. Occasionally two to three foot standing waves from the northeast will build to four and five feet as they squeeze into the narrowing ledges at both sides of the cove.

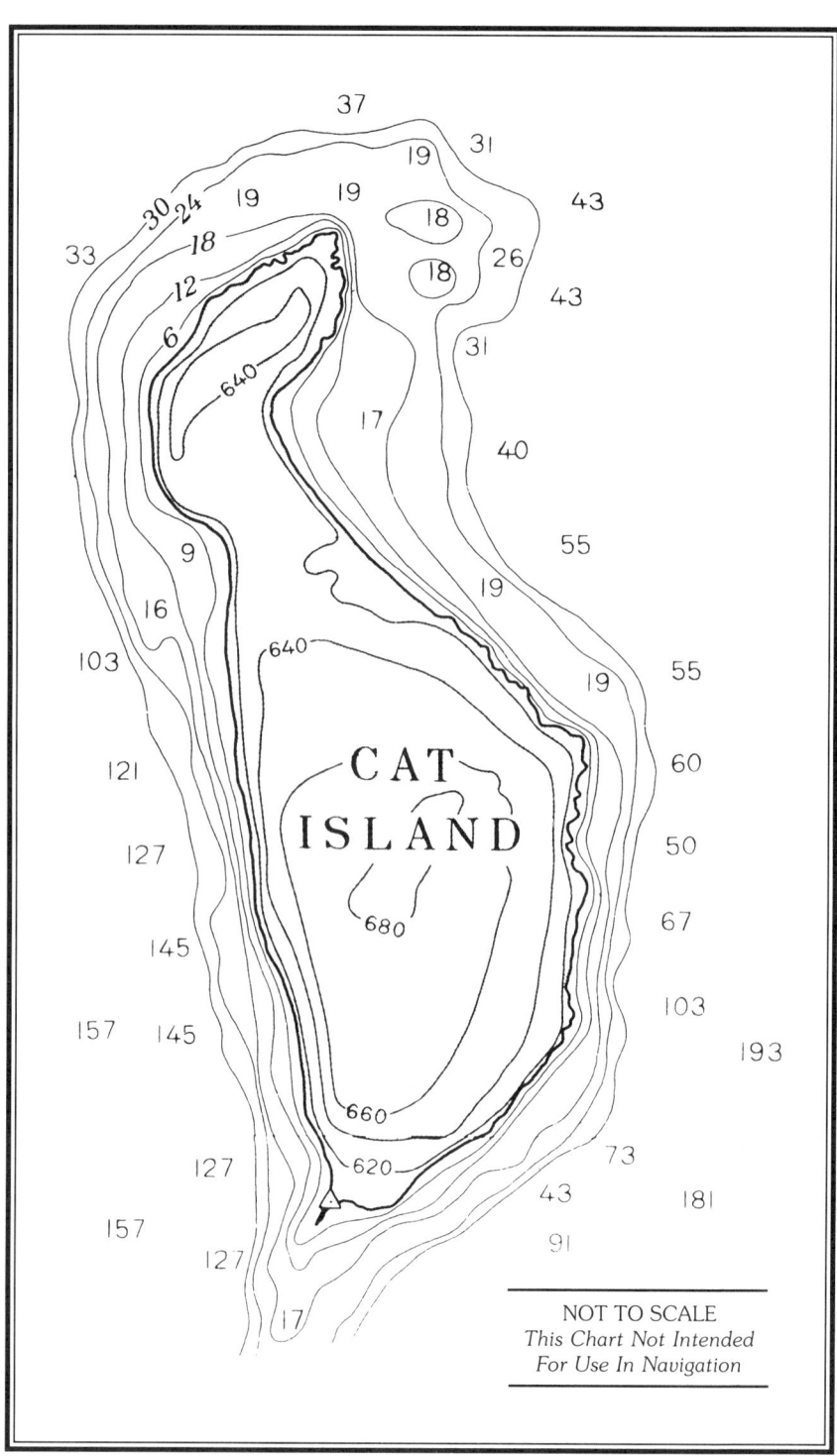

Cat Island

Former Names:
Chippewa name – kagagiwanjikag miniss (Island of Hemlock Trees). Schoolcraft's name – Texas. Local name – Hemlock. Combined local name – Catterhemlock. Other name – Shoe.

Size:
1,348 acres, about 3 miles north to south, narrow neck at the north end, a mile wide in the south end. One name suggests it is shaped like a shoe, but either shapes and styles have changed considerably in footwear since its naming, or their sample shoe had fallen on some pretty rough times. In all fairness, the shoe profile might be seen from the northeast of southwest, even under sober conditions.

Characteristics of the Island:
Part of this island was logged over in the mid-1950's. The island is completely reforested, some of it quite thickly. Though trails are shown on the topographical maps of the mid-1960's, undergrowth and windfalls tangle the former logging trails. The island is low, rising about 80 feet above the lake level. Wave-washed rocky ledges are found off the north end. A

Lake Carriers deliver coal and gravel to Ashland docks and can be found anchored among the islands in rough weather.

picturesque sand spit is found at the south end. South of the northeast corner of the island is a thin beach extending a few hundred feet. A fish camp was located here in former years and a trail extended from that camp to a pickup point on the west side, probably to allow the resident fishermen to exit the island regardless of wind and wave direction.

Moorage and Docking:

There are no docks on the island but the beach at the south end allows easy beaching. The sand bar extending from the sand point drops off gradually to the south, thus allowing a good anchorage on the bar, but drops off abruptly to the west.

Waters Surrounding the Island:

A shelf gradually sloping to 20 feet edges Cat Island. Once beyond this shelf, the depths drop abruptly on the west side of the island, a little less so on the east side.

Fisheries:

A good trout trolling fishery can be found off the island along the west side, around the north tip and back down the east side of the island. Trolling is also done from the northwest side of the island to the south and east side of North Twin Island.

Camping:

Primitive camping can be done on Cat Island, the better locations being the sand point at the south end and a clearing on the northwest part of the island.

The Vicinity:

Four miles to the east of Cat, Outer Island runs 6 miles north and south. Trout Point on Stockton Island is about $2\frac{1}{4}$ miles south of Cat. Ironwood is about 2 miles west, with South Twin about 3 miles to the northwest. North Twin Island lies a mile and a half north of "Catterhemlock."

A typical Apostle Islands beach.

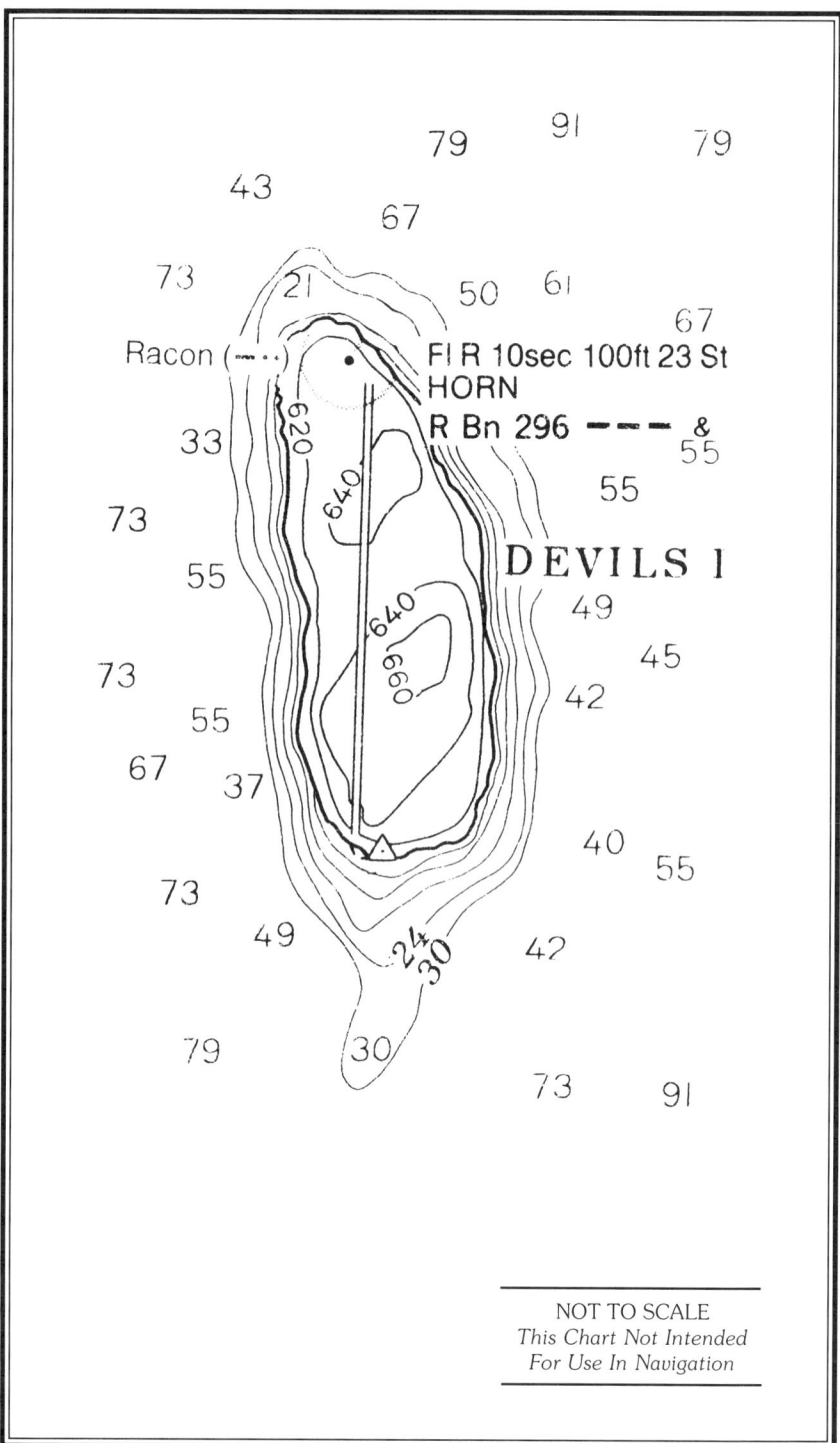

Devils Island

Former Names:
Chippewa name – metchimanitou miniss (Evil Spirit Island). Schoolcraft's name – Louisiana. Other names – Rabbit, Barney, Lamborn's and Brownstone.

Size:
318 acres, $1\frac{1}{4}$ miles long, $\frac{1}{2}$ mile wide.

Devils Island light tower is the youngest and brightest of the six island lights, with a red flash visible 18 miles. The original 1901 crystal fresnel lens is shown in place in the tower. The working red acrylic lens is outside the enclosure.

Characteristics of the Island:
Devils Island is the northernmost point of land in Wisconsin. It rises about 60 feet above water level and is a uniformly rounded island. Most notable about the island, other than its remoteness, are the sea caves which undercut the shoreline. In some places, sometimes, small craft can enter the caves, people can disembark and climb inside the caves up to the turf above. In some places, the sandstone cliffs on the northern half of the island look honeycombed, sometimes even lacy, on a grand scale. The caves occasionally extend back 60 to 70 feet beneath the island. Under severe wave conditions, some former Coast Guardsmen who manned the light until 1978, reported "blow holes" in the surface of the island where pressure escaped as waves bored into the bottleneck-shaped caves. A road extends from the boathouse at the south end of the island to the lighthouse complex on the north end. Along the length of the island hundreds of species of plants compete for sun, space and security. Brush along the trail is extremely tangled and thick, a perfect habitat for the numerous rabbits which make Devils their home. The interior of the island is wet, because of

Devils Island keepers quarters are used by Park Service volunteers who care for the grounds and greet visitors to the lightstation.

the clay soil over the sandstone. The tenacity of the forest is apparent in the ragged and tattered trees which hold their own against the storm forces of the seasons. Some pines on the island date back over 300 years, never having been cut during the logging because of the phenomenon known by loggers and sawyers as "wind shake," a quality of the trunk which shows long twisted cracks in the wood fibers once planks are sawn. The result is poor material. Trees found along the windy shores would exhibit cracked qualities and were not cut.

Historic Sites:

The Devils Island Light Station includes two large lightkeeper's quarters, several smaller buildings which housed equipment and supplies and the tall white steel tower. The cylindrical-shaped tower, standing 80 feet above ground level, was completed in 1898, and illuminated in 1901, replacing a temporary frame tower and lantern used before completion of the main structure. The U.S. Lighthouse Board considered the Devils Island light as one of the most important navigation turning points on Lake Superior. Shortly after it was built, a foghorn was added. In 1978, the Devils Island light was completely automated and the five-man Coast Guard unit was removed from the island. During summer months, the National

Park Service stations volunteer keepers on the island to assist visitors and to protect the structures. At present, the alternating red and white flashing 400,000 candlepower light can be seen for 18 statute miles.

In 1928, Devils Island hosted one of its most famous visitors, President Calvin Coolidge, who toured the islands and stopped for a luncheon picnic on the rock ledges southeast of the sight station. The cement slab the President's table was secured to still remains.

Every year since 1960, thousands of people have viewed the famous Devils Island caves from the excursion boat which passes before the island daily during the summer months.

Another site associated with the lighthouse is the boathouse at the south landing. A small harbor protects the boathouse from waves coming in off the open lake. A clay road, corduroy in some places through the wet parts of the island, runs from the boathouse to the lighthouse complex.

Gunk holing among the Devils Island Seacaves.   *Claire Duquette photo*

Moorage and Docking:

The small harbor at the south end of Devils Island serves well under most sea conditions. The dock extends 175 feet from land to the end of the outermost rock pile on the west side. Sixty feet of the inside of the dock is useable on the west side, with depths from 5 feet to 3 feet. On the same side, nearer the boathouse, a 32 foot jog allows for a shallow draft boat. The east arm of the harbor is generally not useable for tying boats without unusual contrivances of lines and fenders. The bottom here is flat sandstone, and does not allow anchoring. Water is typically clear as one enters the harbor, so rocks are very visible. The boater should bear in mind that the storm conditions out here sometimes move bottom boulders. The arrangements of breakwaters are, by necessity, less orderly than the neat structure of an on-land facility.

The Northeast Landing of natural rock, where Calvin Coolidge's picnic took place, is a very temporary tentative landing with plenty of water depth, but the boater must be prepared to use make-shift fenders and tie-down arrangements. Caution must be used, as rock outcroppings are found here and there. This landing was occasionally used to drop equipment and supplies by the Coast Guard to their men in the station. It was also used by the excursion boats, from time to time, to drop "packages" for the men. The CHIPPEWA would radio the Devils Island Light, indicating it was dropping off a package. The boat would edge into the dock and a suitcase and the "package" – in the person of a girlfriend – would hop ashore to visit her favorite Coast Guardsman. It can be a very good landing, under the right conditions.

NPS curator repairs damage on the Devils Island third order fresnel lens. Reinstalled 1992.

A vessel tied up off this landing should not be left unattended as occasional waves from the wake of passing ships can come in unexpectedly.

Waters Surrounding the Island:

The water depths off the island drop abruptly. The main concern of a boater should be boulders in the water beneath cliffs. Owing to the clarity of the water, rocks appear closer than in water nearer the mainland. Caution should be taken when approaching the south landing as a few boulders might be strewn about the bottom.

Fisheries:

Trolling for lake trout is good off the north end of Devils Island. A mile east of the light is the location of the Devils Island shoals, another notable trolling area.

Camping:

Limited camping is available on Devils Island. Due to the lack of the space, the National Park Service will allow only 2 camping parties.

Trails:

Other than the road from the south dock to the light station, several utility trails lead from the light station to landings, cliffs and overlooks. Hikers should be aware of cliffs all along the periphery of the island.

The Vicinity:

Thirty to 50 miles of the north shore of Lake Superior can be seen stretching out in the distance. Thirty-five miles north of Devils Island is Taconite Harbor, Minnesota, and 30 miles northwest is Silver Bay, Minnesota. Radar domes, towers and stacks can also be seen along this shore. Ore ships and salt water ships can be seen in the shipping channels 6 and 12 miles north of Devils Island. Seventy-five miles west of Devils are the twin ports of Duluth and Superior. Sand Island lies 11 miles southwest of Devils, with Bear Island a little west of south, $2^1/_2$ miles distant. Rocky Island lies about 2 miles southeast. To the east, more a twin to Devils than South Twin, sits North Twin Island. Fifteen miles to the east can be seen the north tip of Outer Island. Ninety-five miles to the northeast lies Isle Royale. Lake Superior stretches 310 miles east from Devils Island.

A gill net tug is designed to withstand a great variety of weather from spring breakup to freeze-up in December.

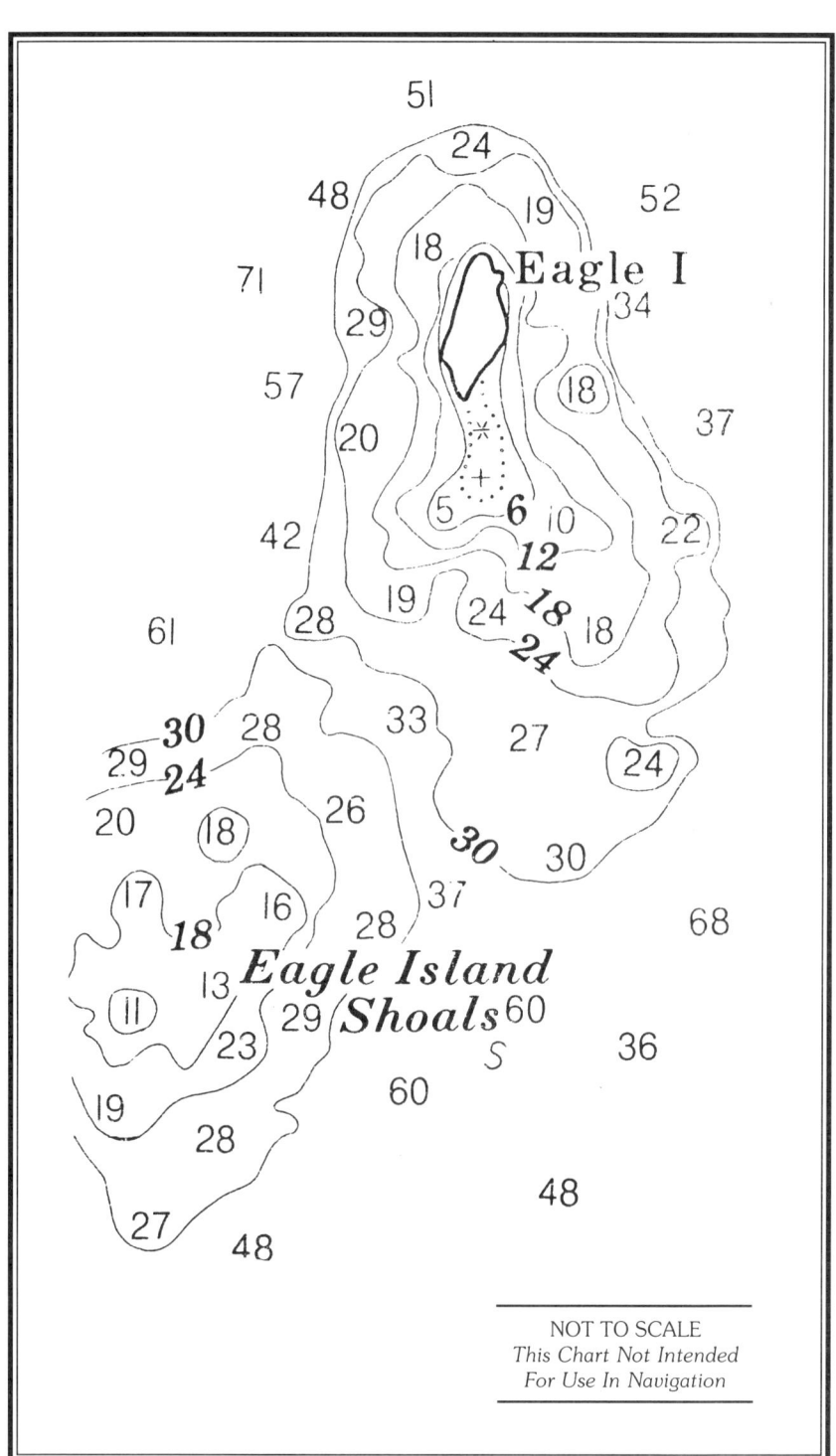

Eagle Island

Former Names:
Chippewa name – nabikwana (Boat Island). Schoolcraft's name – Vermont. Local name – Steamboat Island.

Size:
28 acres.

Characteristics of the Island:
Eagle Island, on the west end of the island group, is the primary nesting site for herring gulls. There is also a great blue heron rookery here. Access and approach to the island are restricted during the nesting periods as visitors will disturb the birds. Access to the island is also dangerous because submerged boulders and reefs generally surround the island.

Fishing:
Trolling for lake trout is often done around Eagle Island and the Eagle Island shoals, as well as off the north end of Sand Point on the mainland.

Camping and Hiking:
No camping or hiking is allowed on Eagle Island by virtue of its use by nesting birds as a nesting site. It is an ecologically sensitive area.

The Vicinity:
South of Eagle Island lies a shoal which used to be Little Steamboat Island up until 1890. A season of unusually powerful storms eroded the top off this small island. A story circulates that a former landowner of Little Steamboat came back to the area to see his property about three years after it had eroded away, not having been notified of its disappearance. The loss of land was bad enough, but tax assessors had let him continue to pay his real estate taxes faithfully for those three years after his land had sunk beneath the surface of the lake.

On the mainland south of Eagle can be found some of the most beautiful sandstone caves of Squaw Bay, along the south shore of the lake.

Waters Surrounding the Island:
Except in calm waters, when a lookout should be posted, approach to the island is dangerous. As mentioned earlier, access is also restricted by the National Park Service. Directly south of Eagle, rocks lie near the surface for a long distance away from the island. The Eagle Island Shoals are of little

concern to shallow draft boats.
　　Sunsets over Eagle are varied and breath-takingly beautiful.

Bald eagles nest among the islands and have been successfully reproducing for several years.

Herring gulls following a fish boat for easy handouts.   Dave Strzok photo

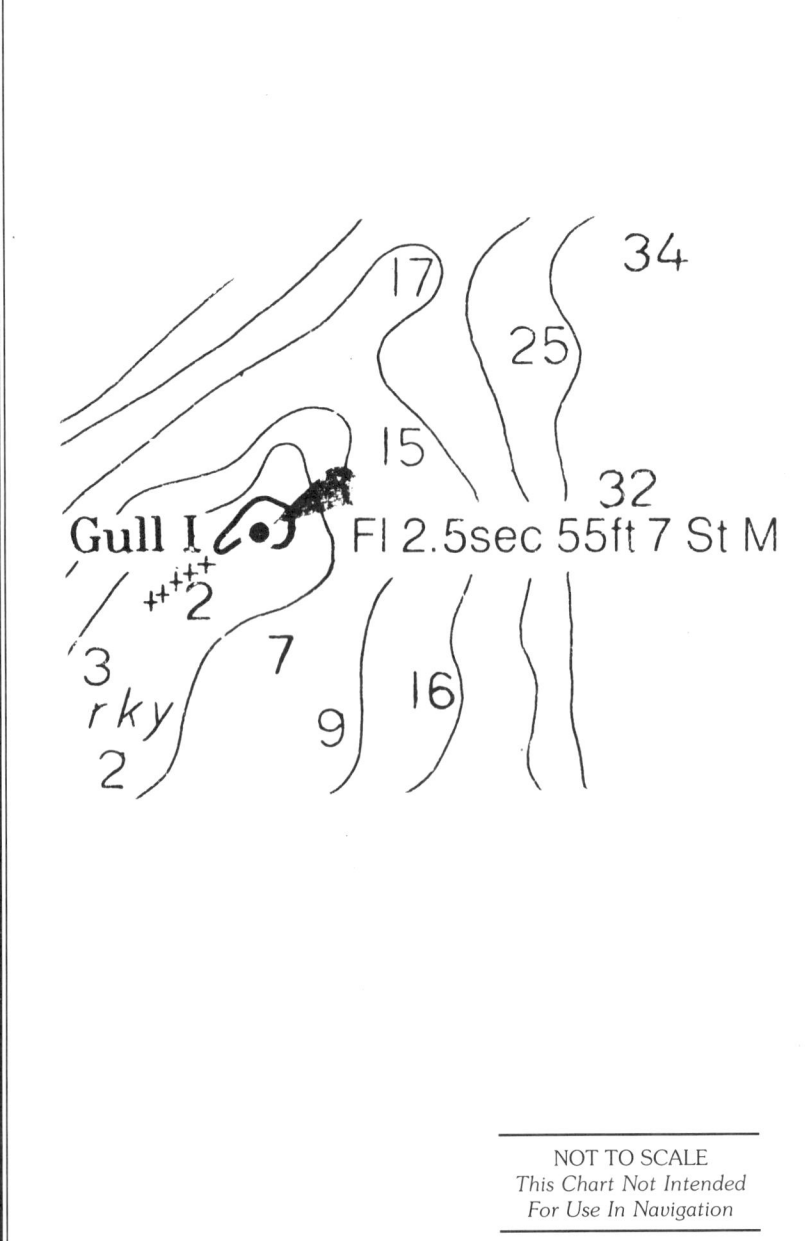

Gull Island

Former Name:
Chippewa name – giashko miniss (Gull Island).

Size:
Three acres.

Characteristics of the Island:
Gull Island is the visible end of a reef extending eastward from Michigan Island. Gull Island's 20 by 200 yard length is covered with various rocks, a swatch of tough grasses, a few ragged trees, countless seagull feathers and abundant evidence that seagulls spend a lot of leisure time. In fact, when approaching downwind of the island on a hot summer day, the evidence is overwhelming.

An automatic white navigation light warns of reefs surrounding the island and also serves as a range light for ships entering Chequamegon Bay via the South Channel.

Visitation to Gull Island is restricted as it is one of the primary nesting sites of the herring gull. During the nesting period, from latter May to the end of June, boaters may not approach the island as the intrusion unsettles nesting birds.

Waters Surrounding the Island:
This island is surrounded by reefs, the most extensive one lying submerged just beneath the surface between Gull and Michigan Island. Though shallow draft boats might be able to pick a route across the reef under ideal weather conditions, casual cruising is not advised in this area.

Historical Site:
In spite of its forlorn appearance today, this island used to have a dock and fish camp.

Fisheries:
The reefs around Gull Island supply excellent habitat for spawning fish and are considered important areas for fish reproduction in the lake. For this reason, sport fishing restrictions in this area are often in effect. Sport fishermen should check with the Wisconsin Department of Natural Resources for current regulations on fishing.

The Vicinity:

When seen from Julian Bay on Stockton Island Gull Island sometimes appears to be a stationary ship anchored northeast of Michigan Island. Very young observers with unshackled imaginations occasionally see Gull Island as a spouting whale resting half in and half out of the water. They should check with the Wisconsin Department of Natural Resources for current regulations on whaling.

Herring gulls and ring-billed gulls nest among the islands.

Lookout point on Hermit Island.

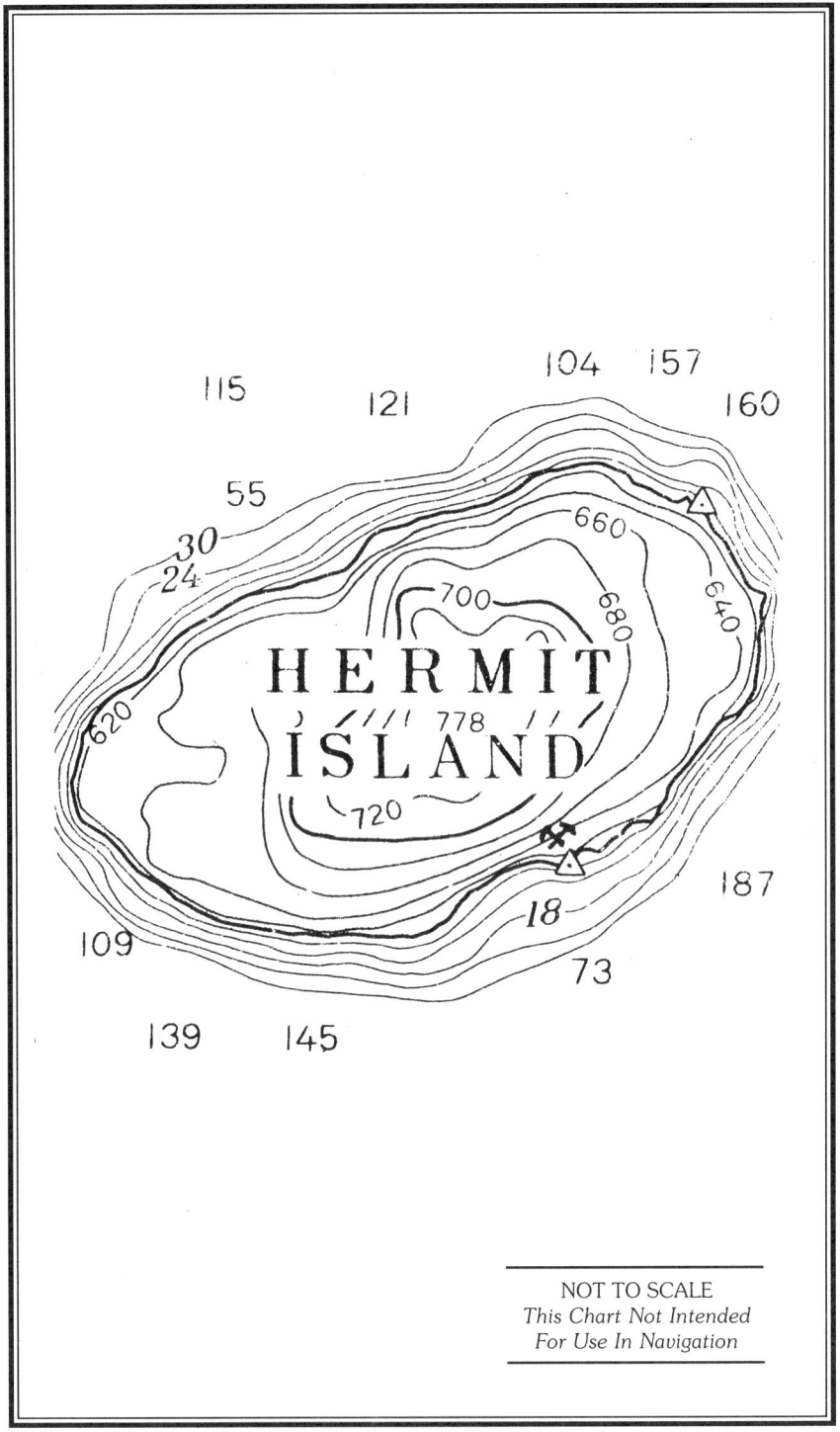

Hermit Island

Former Names:
Chippewa name – ashuwaguidag miniss (The Further Island). Schoolcraft's name – Minnesota. Local name – Wilson's Island. Former name – Askew.

Size:
778 acres, about two miles long, $3/4$ mile wide, about 160 feet above lake level.

Characteristics of the Island:
Hermit Island is roughly egg-shaped. The shores rise steeply except for two drainage ravines at the northwest and north sides, and the quarry site along the southeast shore. Beaches can be found along the southwest shore and at the drainage midway along the north shore. Clay banks rise to the forest of mixed hardwoods, cedars and pines along most of the west two-thirds of the island. Scenic rocky cliffs rise up from the shore on the northwest third of the island where the effects of easterly and northeasterly storms carve shelves and abrupt formations in the sandstone. The sea cliffs are particularly beautiful along the southeast and east ends of the island where one will find points jutting out from the cliffs and huge rocks tumbled down. "Lookout Point" used to arch over a hole in the cliff until nature's processes caused it to tumble on a summer day in 1975.

Historic Sites:

Hermit Island's history is colorful and varied. One amateur archeologist recalls reading British Colonial Papers which describe a small outpost on steep clay banks at a time when intruders were unwelcome. The outpost was allegedly destroyed by Indians along with some of the handful of soldiers who manned the post. According to popular stories, a cooper named Wilson moved to the island after he was banned from Madeline Island following a quarrel with "King" John Bell in the early 1840's. Wilson had challenged Bell's leadership which was based on strength, influence and basic politics. This leadership arrangement was universal in North American territories before statehood, and challengers were a normal part of the scheme of things in those days. After a day-long fist fight, Wilson conceded to Bell and was, as a result, banned from Madeline Island. Taking up residence on Wilson's Island, Wilson lived there in relative reclusiveness until he was found dead in his bed by Indian agent Benjamin Armstrong and his wife who had come to visit him in the early 1850's. According to the tale, Wilson's cabin had been ransacked, suggesting foul play by someone wishing to help himself to whatever hoard of money Wilson had stashed on the island.

Another story circulates that a cache of silver and gold might have been hidden on the island during the time that French soldiers manned Grant's Point fort. The story goes that the paymaster, coming from French headquarters eastward, was arriving in the Apostle Islands region late in the day. Rather than land at LaPointe unannounced and risking being recog-

One of Hermit Island's two stone quarries. Among other late 1800s buildings, the Detroit Chamber of Commerce building material came from this quarry.

nized by the criminal element, the paymaster elected to spend the night on Hermit Island and to arrive in LaPointe very early in the morning the next day. During the night, the payroll estimated at about $8,000 (and since redoubling in value many times over), was stolen and hidden. The paymaster was unable to elicit a confession and retrieve the money. Treasure hunters over the years have gouged and scoured the probable hiding places but none have reported finding it. If any treasure does in fact exist, it will rest in peace, belonging to all of us, as National Park Service regulations prohibit such searching.

In the latter part of the 19th century, a quarry was opened on Hermit Island. As many as a hundred workmen quarried the site on the south side of the island. A hotel housed the workers until the latter part of the 1900's when quarrying was no longer profitable. The owner of the operation, Frederick Prentice, had built an elaborate cottage called "The Cedar Bark Lodge" in the 1890's. Appointments in the cottage were impressive, including a carved sandstone fireplace and, for himself and his guests, a third story lookout for their viewing pleasure. The tale goes that Prentice married a young society lady of 19 years of age from his native New York City. Rumor says that, upon arriving on Hermit Island she took

Hermit Island quarry, one of three quarries operated among the islands between 1868 and the early 1900s.

one look around and refused to live there in such surroundings, making her way back the same day. The cottage was left to be used by Prentice's friends. It was eventually dismantled in the early 1930's, the fireplaces being re-installed in a home in Bayfield.

In 1910, an enterprise in the Minneapolis area attempted to subdivide and establish lots for sale surrounding a fruit plantation. Each landowner, according to the brochure describing the settlement, would enjoy a cool vista of the lake and would be placed in such a fashion that privacy was assured. Streets were named and plotted. The venture failed and the developers went on to other projects. Since those days, private landowners not associated with the development have built cabins on several sites on the island.

During the 1900's, a homestead was developed above the cliffs on the southeast side. The farmer planted a pear and apple orchard where remnant trees can be found at present.

Moorage and Docking:

Tentative anchorages are possible off the sand beach extending along the south coast of the island up to the rock cliffs at the east. Rocks will be found in the water but the bottom is primarily sand or sand and mud. These anchorages are good when favored by the wind. An anchorage can also be used off the drainage and beach midway on the north coast of the island where the bottom is sand. Obvious consideration should be given to wind direction. Beaching a power boat is also possible along the sand beaches described above, with consideration for boulders at each extremity of the beaches. Shallow draft boats can also be brought in along shore near the quarry site though a lookout should watch for large boulders fallen from rock ledges.

A landing is also possible north of the west extremity of the island near a drainage, though rocks and a cobble bottom must be watched.

Waters Surrounding the Island:

Below the cliffs on the east shore of the island, the depths drop off abruptly. A shelf extends out from the northeast corner of the island, with dangerous boulders off the point northwest of Lookout Point. Depths around the north side of the island drop off gradually and can be approached cautiously. Cobbles along the west and southwest of the island call for caution. The large boulders off the cliffs on the south and southeast should be watched close to shore.

Fisheries:
Winter bobbing for lake trout is often done along the south shore of Hermit Island through the ice.

Camping:
Camping is allowed along the north shore of the island west of the drainage and beach. Camps can also be located inland from the beach found along the south and west half of the island. Camping may not be done near the quarry.

Trails:
Short trails lead from the drainage on the west side of the island a few hundred yards inland. Trees on much of the western two-thirds of the island are mature enough to allow cross-country hiking on Hermit Island.

The Vicinity:
To the south of Hermit Island, is Madeline Island two and a half miles across the North Channel. Stockton is a mile and a half east of Hermit. Oak Island rises about a mile and three-quarters to the north. Between Stockton and Oak Island one can see Manitou Island four miles distant. The mainland at Red Cliff Point can be seen two and a half miles west of Hermit Island. One and a half miles southeast of Hermit lies Basswood Island.

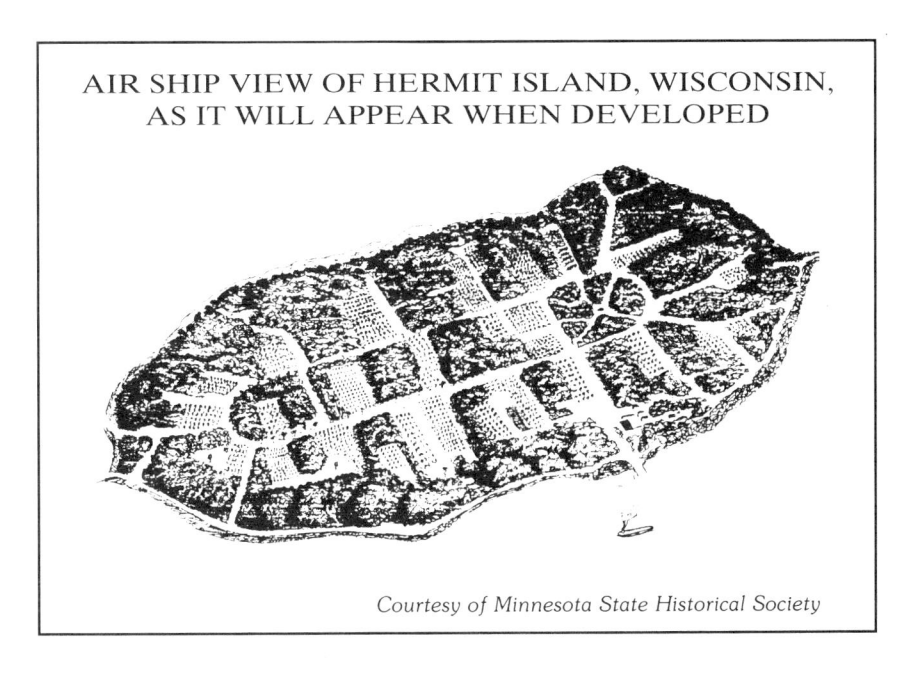

AIR SHIP VIEW OF HERMIT ISLAND, WISCONSIN, AS IT WILL APPEAR WHEN DEVELOPED

Courtesy of Minnesota State Historical Society

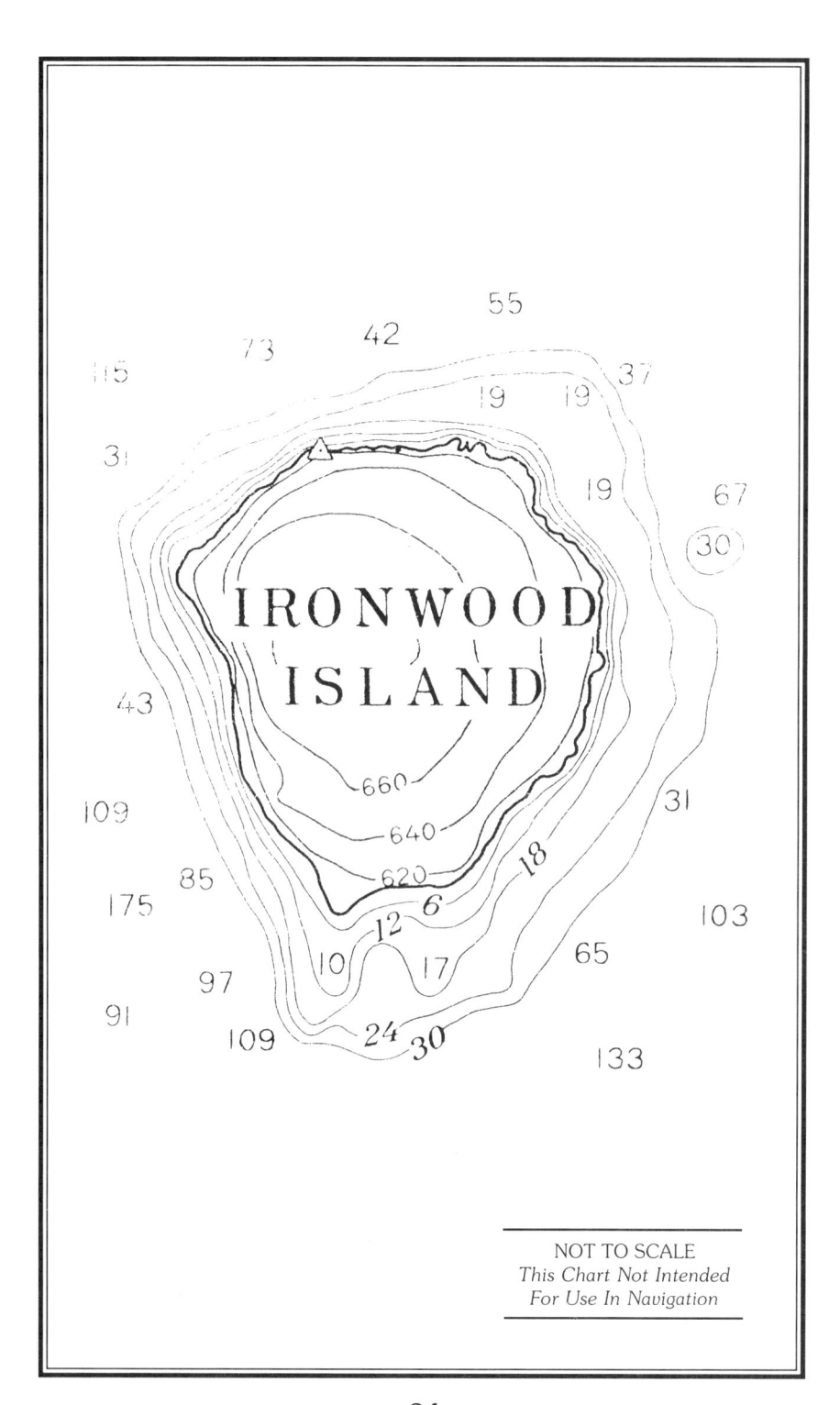

IRONWOOD ISLAND

NOT TO SCALE
This Chart Not Intended For Use In Navigation

34

Ironwood Island

Former Names:
Chippewa name – gemananosi miniss (Island of the Ironwood Trees). Schoolcraft's name – North Carolina. Other name – Higgin's.

Size:
659 acres, about one mile across, $1\frac{1}{4}$ miles north to south.

Characteristics of the Island:
Ironwood Island rises gradually to about 80 feet above the lake level. It is forested with conifers and hardwoods, but used to be a forest of ironwood trees before the island was cut for its timber. The island was most recently logged in the early 1950's. A sand spit marks the south end of the island.

Historic Sites:
Logging and fishing shelters were located on the south point for use during the logging days of the 1950's and the fishing era before that.

Moorage and Docking:
An anchorage in shallow water is possible south of the sand point where a bar extends a considerable distance out. The bar drops off sharply to the east and west of the sand bar. Beaching a boat along the point is the best means of access to the island, although approach should be slow because the bar can be quite shallow far from the beach.

Waters Surrounding the Island:
As in most cases among the islands, rocky ledges face north, occasionally northeast and northwest. Such is the case on Ironwood Island. Off the south end of the island, the bottom rises abruptly. A pond net is often placed off the west side of the sand point.

Camping:
At present, there are no designated campsites. However the most desirable location for camping is on the sand point. There are no facilities, so considerate outdoor practices should be used.

Hiking:
Though 1964 topographical maps show trails lacing the island, at present it is overgrown with about 40 year's growth of forest.

The Vicinity:

About 2½ miles south of Ironwood is the 7-mile-long north coast of Stockton Island. Two miles west is Cat Island. North about four miles is North Twin Island. Northeast two and three miles are South Twin and Rocky Islands respectively. West lies Otter; southwest is Manitou Island.

> **MADELINE ISLAND**
>
> To the east is Madeline Island, known to the Ojibway as Moningwunakauning, "The Home of the Golden Breasted Woodpecker." The French soldier Pierre le Sueur built his post there in 1693. In 1718 a fort was erected which remained France's principal fur-trading post on Lake Superior until New France fell to the English. In 1793 Michel Cadotte established a trading post and began permanent settlement. When Equaysayway, daughter of Chief White Crane and a member of the Ojibway aristocracy, married Michel Cadotte, she was given the Christian name "Madeleine." Her pleased father declared the island should be named in her honor.
>
> Erected 1956

Madeline Island is the only Apostle Island not part of the National Lakeshore.

Long Island

Chippewa Name- shegawomegon or shakohwamic miniss

Size: 300 acres, about 3.84 miles of the barrier beach

Characteristics: Long Island is now joined to the seven-mile-long sand spit, part of Chequamegon Point, which originates near the mouth of the Bad River on the mainland. Its most recent joining with the long barrier beach occurred in the 1970's. At one time, Indians described the distance between the island proper and the sand point as "the length an arrow would fly before it fell to earth."

Waters surounding the Island:

Sand shifts so much on the island-spit that little can be said about its present depths. Barrier shallows come up to two feet in some places and drop back to five feet in some places. The next week, everything has changed. The water usually becomes shallow within a hundred yards of the island. However, the channel between Madeline Island and Long island is deep, crated by a swift current of water circulating through the passage between the islands. From the days of the original 1860's lighthouse, whose remains can be found midway on the east/west segment of the island, the beach has extended north over 300 feet. The western tip of the island shows severe recent erosion which necessitated the relocation of the LaPointe Light and its replacement in 1988. The new white cylindrical tower is simply functional, nothing as esthetically pleasing as the old tower

LaPointe Lightstation served as site of U.S. Coast Guard until the 1960's. The dock will be removed in 1999 by the National Park Service..

which was decommissioned and placed back among the trees after being air-lifted about 200 feet and replanted by a US Coast Guard helicopter.

Historic Sites:

The history of Long Island goes back in Indian legend to the formation of the island group, to the story of Winnibijou pursuing and attempting to entrap ammik, the beaver, in the "soft mud dam," Chequamegon Point.

Significant Indian wars took place on Long Island between the Sioux/Fox contingent and the Chippewa/Ottawa groups, with no dates supplied by people who do not regard dates as significant.
The earliest French outpost of the 1690's were on "La Pointe" of Long Island. Within a few yars, the early French established a favorable rapport with the Madeline Island Chippewa, eventually moving their outpost to Grants Point on the southwest tip of Madeline Island.

The first lighthouse of the Apostle Islands was supposed to be built on Long Island in 1857, but the builder was apparently pursuaded by local shippers to build the lighthouse on Michigan Island. When the lighthouse inspector discovered the discrepency, he insisted a light tower be built on Long Island, which was then built between the present two light towers and was illuminated in 1858. An additional light was established in 1895, at the present location, as well as a 40-foot light tower and a striking bell at the western tip of the point. In 1938, the US Coast Guard created a station at the eastern tower site, where a Coast Guard contingent manned the station until 1964, when the lights were automated and the Coast Guard detachment moved to the mainland.

Recent History:

Long Island was added to the National Lakeshore in 1987. Due to the nature of the "island" as a barrier spit, the National Park decided to complete a number of studies before proceeding with planning for its use. Most of those have now been completed including geomorphology, basic biology, archaeology, some ethnology, and a few studies related to specific issues. The Park Service is prepared to create a Long Island plan, however, it is not a high priority because the process is not funded and it is a very high probability that the use and development will not change much from the current state. The shallow approaches and beaches make it a good place for small boat picnics and any substantial dock would have major environmental impact on the shoreline. Additional preservation and trail and walk restoration may be taken and the stabilization of the old light on the point is in the park program a couple of years away.[1999]

A few facts or things recent studies verified are:

1. The spit is slowly moving toward the Lake, building sand on the Lakeside and losing it on the bay side. This was, of course, fairly evident from the fact that the site of the original lighthouse is much farther inland from it's original orientation from lake and the original foundations for the light on the point are now pretty much in the bay.

2. The island contains critical habitat for the endangered Piping Plover. There was a successful nest in the summer of 1998, the first successful one in the State of Wisconsin in over ten years. (The last successful one was also on Long Island) The nests, which are largely unprotected except by coloration on the beach are very sensitive to any kind of traffic. (Including the occasional 4 wheelers that make it out from the mainland)

3. The island has been invaded fairly heavily by Purple Loosestrife (currently the only such infestation in the park). Efforts to contain the invasion by chemical applications and physical removal of plants have been largely unsuccessful. The Park Service is currently raising and using a biological control (beetles) to attack the problem. [1999]

The Lucerne sank against Long Island in an 1886 storm in the Apostle Islands. The Lucerne is one of several underwater sites being surveyed for nomination to the National Register of Historic places. (Illustration courtesy of the Milwaukee Public Libary Great Lakes Marine Historical Collection)

NOT TO SCALE
*This Chart Not Intended
For Use In Navigation*

Manitou Island

Former Names:
Chippewa name – manitou miniss (Spirit Island). Schoolcraft's name – New Jersey. Former names – Devil's, Tate's.

Size:
1,363 acres, about $2\frac{1}{2}$ miles long, 1 mile wide, 120 feet of elevation above the lake level.

Historical Sites:
One of the most complete fish camps on the Apostle Islands is located on Manitou Island. The camp apparently began in the late 1800's and has been in use until very recently. When the large fishery collection boats were stopping at the islands, the boats went to Sand, Bear, Manitou and Madeline Islands on the same day.

At the present time, about a half-dozen sheds and cabins remain at the southwest corner of the island. Their most recent inhabitant was Hjalmer "Governor" Olson, a fisherman who first fished off Manitou Island in the 1930's.

Waters Surrounding the Island:
The most notable hazard to navigation near Manitou is Little Manitou, a small pile of stone with a flashing navigation light on a small white battery box. Little Manitou marks the end of a shoal which extends from the Manitou shore. In former years (before 1960), the shoal and Little Manitou were a much larger island, 300 feet long, 50 to 75 feet wide and 40 feet high, whose biggest problem was that it was eroding away. Gulls could find adequate housing on Little Manitou (also

Manitou Island Olson fish camp is a stop on excursion cruises.

41

known as Gull Rock, Little Devils, or Pigeon). In the early 1960's, the Coast Guard decided it had to speed up the erosion process to establish a more permanent base for the warning light. The soft over-burnen was washed away with a fire hose, leaving the shoal and a pile of rocks for the light.

Boaters should cruise westward of the light on Little Manitou. Water depths drop off regularly around the rest of Manitou Island.

Moorage and Docking:

Docking along a new Park Service dock is very good, with depths from 7 feet gradually shallowing toward the beach.

Camping and Hiking:

Campers can be delivered by tour boat which visits the island daily in mid-summer. A half-hour visit by excursionists allows visitors to learn about commercial fishing at this site.

A fisherman demonstrates mending nets on Manitou Island.

Built in 1857, this classic lighthouse was built in the wrong place – specified for Long Island, the builder was apparently persuaded to construct it on Michigan Island, rather than Long Island.

44

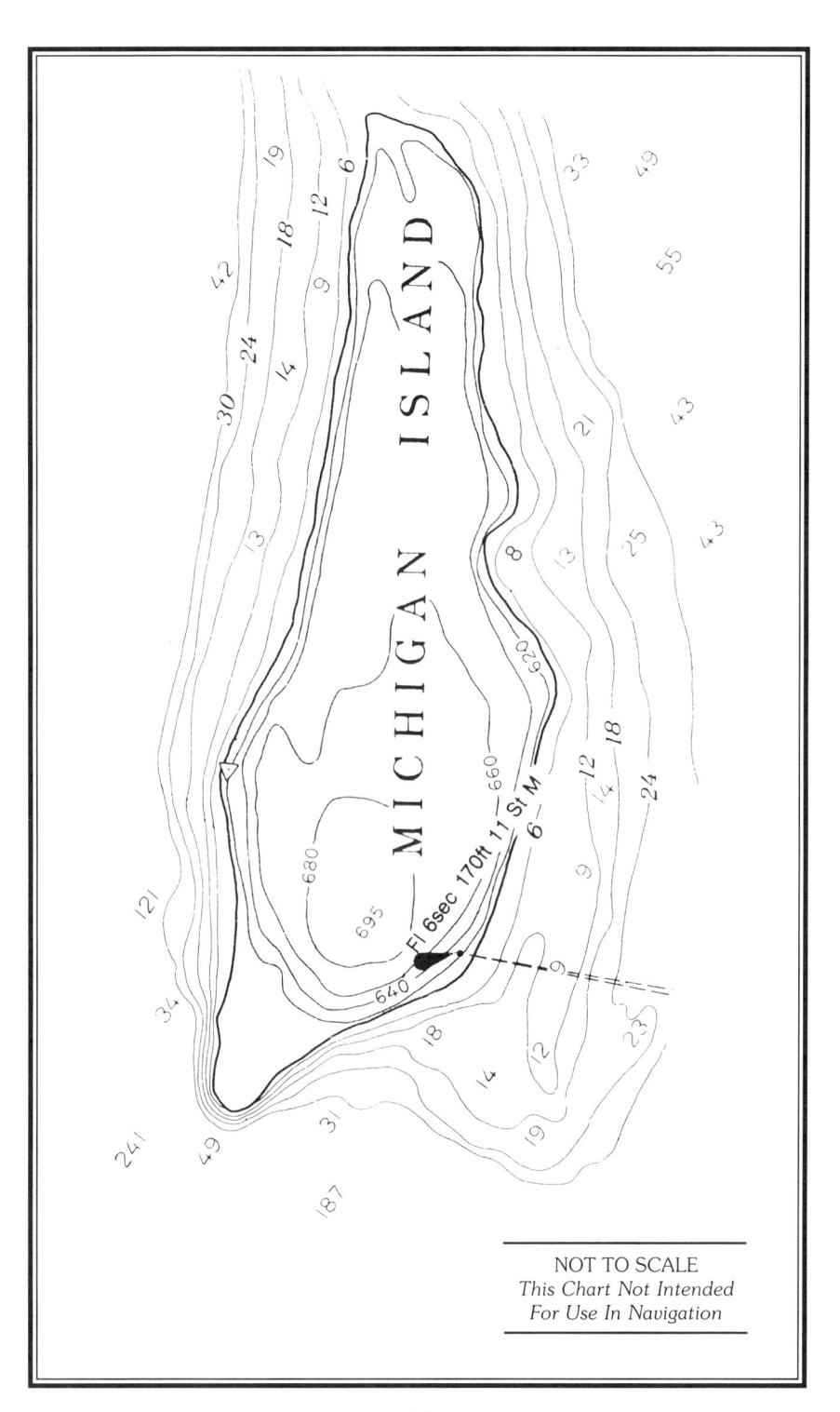

Michigan Island

Former Names:
Chippewa name – bugadabi miniss (Hook and Line Island). Schoolcraft's name – Indiana.

Size:
1,581 acres, $3\frac{1}{2}$ miles long, $1\frac{1}{4}$ miles wide.

Characteristics of the Island:
Michigan Island rises 90 feet above the lake level. The southwest end of the island is a sand spit with long picturesque beaches extending both north and south from the point, with the southern beach extending about a mile. The shores change from beach to clay cliffs for most of the remainder of the island's periphery, except for the northeast end where the island flattens out and the shores are covered with cobbles. Two small ponds can be found a short distance inland behind much shoreline vegetation at both the northeast and southwest ends of the island.

Historic Sites:
Michigan Island has two lights at the southernmost part of the island. These structures are located about a mile east of the sand point. One is an old picturesque brick and masonry tower with lightkeeper's quarters attached. This structure has been stabilized by the National Park Service to prevent deterioration. This lighthouse, built in 1858, was considered too short for a 360° beacon. In 1926, the present steel tower, about 40 feet taller than the narrow masonry tower, was built and now operates automatically. A National Park Service volunteer resides at the light station during the summer and can answer boater's inquiries. A narrow tramway and stairs run up from the shore to the cliff where the lightstation is located.

The steel skeleton tower, 2nd lighthouse, came from Schooner Ledge in 1918, erected 1929, to replace the short 1854 tower.
Photo by C. Johnson

Almost all the history of the island revolves around the lightstation. Families often accompanied lightkeepers to lighthouses, either bringing with them necessities or utilizing resources to meet their needs. A number of years ago, one lightkeeper planted an apple orchard of some 16,000 trees. The trees did not do well and since have been overgrown by natural vegetation.

Moorage and Docking:

Though numerous attempts have been made to establish a dock on Michigan Island, none have permanently withstood the battering of waves against the island in foul weather. Even a concrete "all-weather" pier lies crumbled below the surface off the lighthouse stairs and tramway.

An L-shaped dock was built in the 1980's. Sand drifts readily along this shore and water depths will vary greatly at the dock.

Waters Surrounding the Island:

Navigation charts indicate unusual differences in water depths off Michigan Island: reefs extend to Gull Island off the east end of the island, a relatively shallow shelf lies off the south side of the island, and there is an abrupt drop off at the west end. These factors and the open location of the island conspire to permit more extreme weather changes than one finds in protected waters.

Beachcombers on Michigan Island.

Specific sites requiring precaution include the boulders and crumbled concrete dock a few hundred feet south of the lighthouse. A boater should approach the lighthouse stairs slowly and with a lookout at the bow. At the east end of Michigan Island, a shoal extends to Gull Island 2 to 3 feet beneath the surface. Passage through this area is not advised.

Fisheries:

Sport fishing regulations in the area are subject to change. Sportsmen should seek current information from the Wisconsin Department of Natural Resources.

Camping:

The camper should check with the National Park Service ranger for camp sites. One will find large logs and other driftwood lying in a region of beach grasses. Campers should bear in mind that the beach grass helps keep the sand from blowing away and should be protected from disruption and indiscriminate camp fires. Campers should also keep in mind that the large pieces of driftwood are part of the wild beauty of the beach. Firewood should be selected from deadwood in the woods behind the beach or gathered from loose wood along the beach.

Michigan Island Sand Point.

Trails:

A few logging trails transect the island but are not clearly marked. (See map.)

The Vicinity:

Looking west from the sand point of Michigan Island, one sees the east shore of Madeline Island about 4 miles distant. Slightly to the north of Madeline Island and beyond, one will see the rolling hills of the mainland north of Bayfield, about 15 miles distant, with Hermit and Basswood about 7 and 10 miles away respectively. To the north lies Stockton Island, with Presque Isle Point jutting toward Michigan Island across about $2^1/_2$ miles of channel. During the summer months one will see a regular traffic of boats going to and from the dock and bay west of Presque Isle Point. To the northeast, about 10 miles, lies Outer Island. Out straight east is open Lake Superior. Looking a little south of east, on a clear day one can see the Keweenaw Peninsula of Upper Michigan. A little more to the south, one will see the Porcupine Mountains and, on occasion, the high scaffold of the Copper Peak Ski Flying Jump near Black River Harbor. More to the south, the Gogebic Range near Ironwood, Michigan rolls westward into the Penokee Range of ancient mountains south of Ashland, Wisconsin. In the South Channel toward the southwest, at varying distances, one might see a few trolling boats making their way back and forth in the fishing ground off Chequamegon Point, which is some 17 miles away.

Sailboards skip among the islands from docksites.

Third order fresnel lens from Michigan Island Lighthouse, displayed at Apostle Islands National Lakeshore.

Photo by Claire Duquette

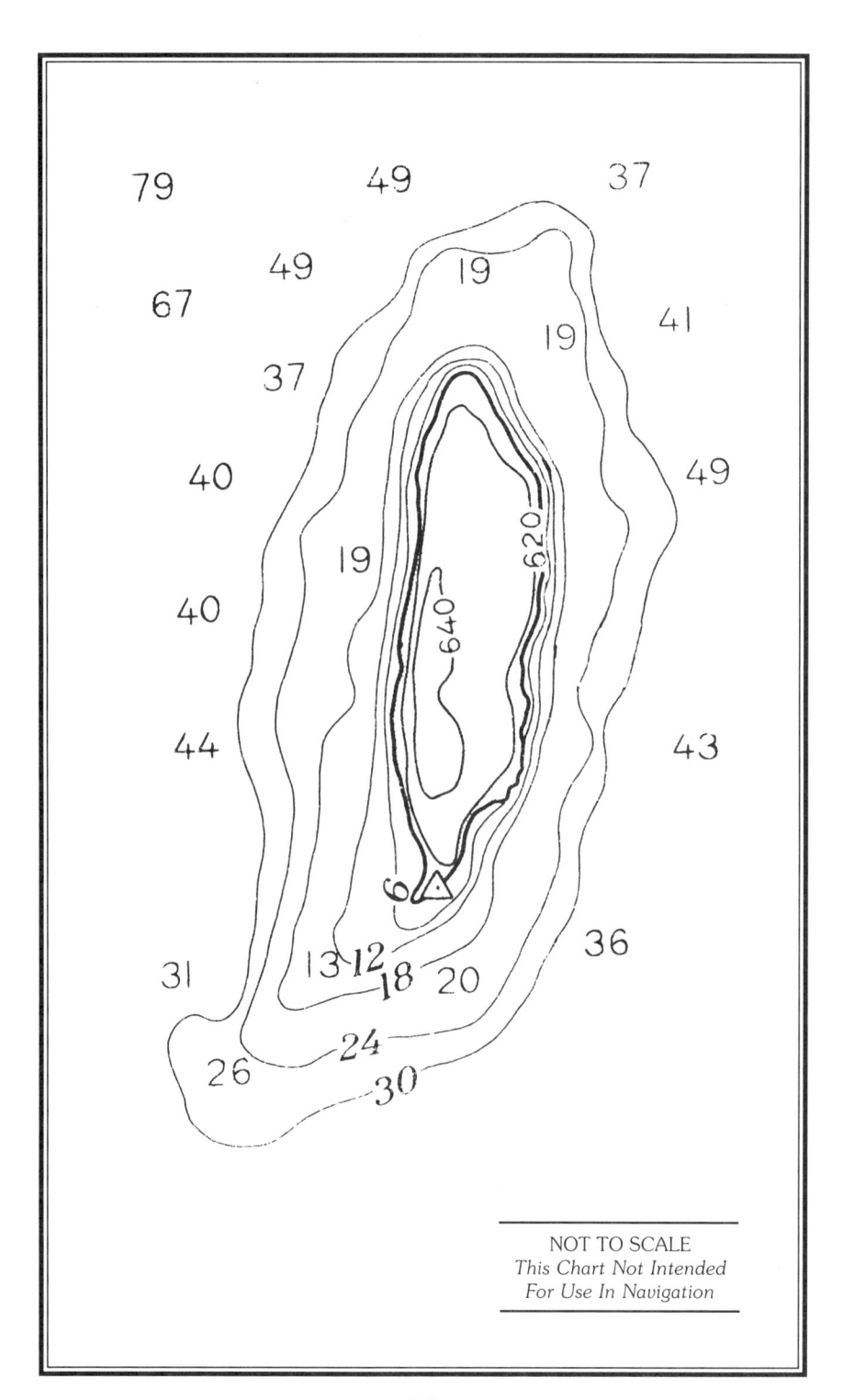

NOT TO SCALE
*This Chart Not Intended
For Use In Navigation*

50

North Twin Island

Former Names:
Chippewa name – miskwassikag miniss (Red Stone Island). Schoolcraft's name – Alabama. Local name – Brownstone. Other name – Cat.

Size:
175 acres, a little more than a mile long, $\frac{1}{4}$ mile wide.

Characteristics of the Island:
North Twin is very similar in shape and foliage to Devils Island, though its "twin" is South Twin. Most of the island is rock with a shallow topping of clay. The clay, remnants of the glacial deposits thousands of years before, is thicker at the south end of the island. Owing to its remoteness from the mainland, and its small size, North Twin Island was not logged as other islands were. Therefore, the island is relatively undisturbed and is considered an example of native boreal forest. In addition, several species of rare vegetation are found on the island. The north shore of the island is rocky ledge, where vegetation seems to be crawling outward but has been rebuffed again and again by the crashing seas that tear at the island in stormy weather.

Moorage and Docking:
Access to the island is difficult. Camping is not permitted on North Twin Island.

Fisheries:
A favorite lake trout trolling area extends along the east and west shores of North Twin, as well as in an arch across the north end of the island. Trolling along the east side extends all the way down to the north end of Cat Island.

The Vicinity:
North Twin rests far out in the lake about equal distance between Devils Island and Outer Island. From the north end of the island, one faces the open lake and the same sights as one sees from Devils Island.

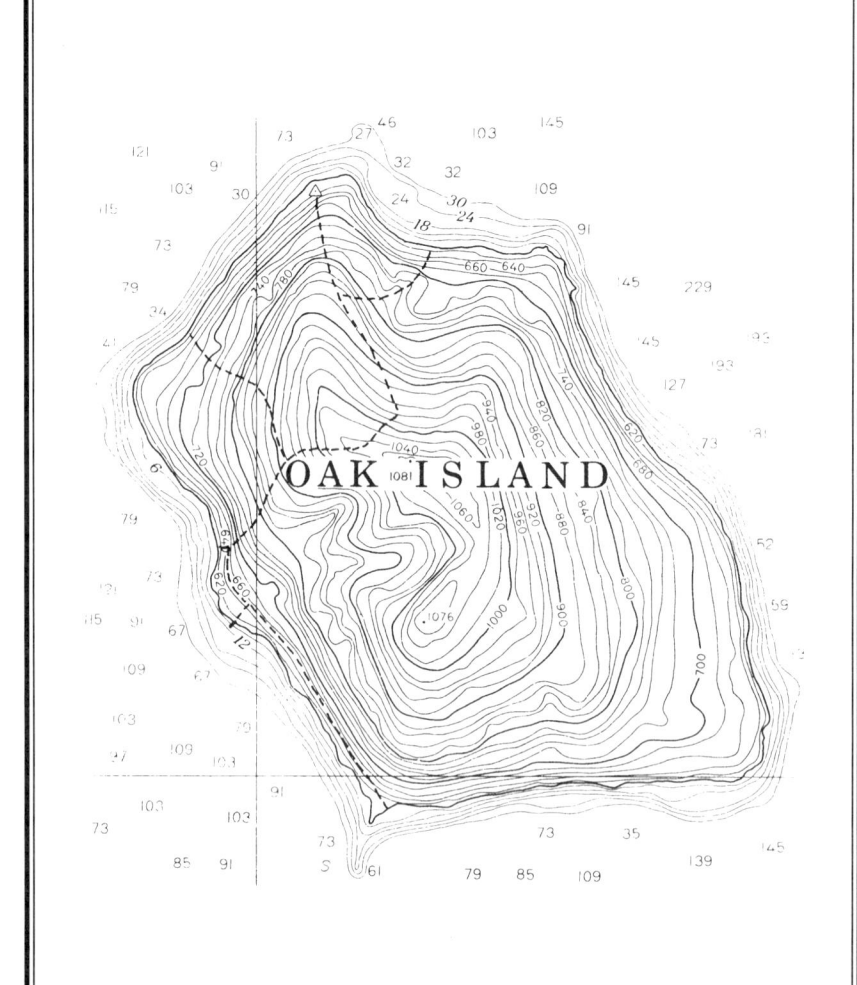

NOT TO SCALE
This Chart Not Intended For Use In Navigation

52

Oak Island

Former Names:
Chippewa name – mitigominkang miniss (Acorn Island). Schoolcraft's name – New York.

Size:
5,078 acres, 4 miles long, 3-3$\frac{1}{2}$ miles wide, 480 feet above lake level.

Characteristics of the Island:
Oak Island is the tallest of the Apostle Islands and is often a landmark for boaters approaching Bayfield and the Chequamegon Bay area. Deep ravines drop down from the tall mass of the island. Between the 1,000 foot and 1,050 foot elevations above sea level, beach lines can be found along what would have been the island's east shoreline about 11,000 years ago. The present trail system passes through a portion of this former beach.

The island is covered with a forest of mixed hardwoods with some stands of conifers. Ground cover varies from dense where foliage competes for the sunlight to relatively mature forest where cross-country hiking is easier. The shoreline on the east side of the island is predominantly scenic sandstone cliffs while the remainder of the coastline is either clay banks or steep forested shore. Beaches can be found at the sand point on the southwest corner of the island, at and near the northwest corner and midway between the southeast corner and southwest sand point. A prominent sandstone point off the northeast corner of the island juts out disclosing an arch of rock with a "window."

Oak beaching point – Sand Spit.

Historic Information:

Shortly after the last glacial period, about 12,000 years ago, Oak Island would have been the only island above the water level. As the level of Lake Superior receded, a beach developed about 1,000 feet above sea level and is still visible to the hiker. History is sketchy until the Chippewa Indians migrated into the region. They may have used Oak Island in maple sugar processing. Legend has it that a band of pirates, called the Twelve Apostles, would beach their boat in the ravines of the island to hide from passing boats. The Twelve Apostles' history was brief but fatal to a few boats and passengers who were captured for their valuables. A newspaper account reprinted during our nation's Bicentennial year tells a story of how the buccaneers were seen beached in Frog Bay which faces Oak Island from the mainland. A passer-by recognized the band of ruffians, reported his sighting to the constabulary on Madeline Island and a group of men set out to capture the Twelve Apostles. The culprits were captured and disposed of in whatever was the popular method of the 18th Century.

During the 1800's, a well-known entrepreneur and steamboat operator logged part of Oak Island and sold his surplus wood to transient steamships to fire their steam boilers. Parts of Oak Island were logged at great risk to horses and men due to the steep slopes. Logs and horses occasionally tumbled down the ravines and hillsides, making logging there particularly hazardous.

In the mid-1800's, Benjamin Armstrong and his wife lived near the southeast sand point on the island. Armstrong had been an Indian agent and was one of the formers of the economy in the Chequamegon area. He was reputed to have been rewarded by grateful Chippewas who led him, blindfolded, about three days southeast of Ashland to a place where he found and picked up gold nuggets lying on the surface of the ground. He apparently wished to return to the place but was subsequently blinded by an explosion of gunpowder that was thrown into his campfire while he was hosting three strangers along a trail between Ashland and Duluth. Though he regained most of his eyesight several years later, he could no longer recognize the place where the gold nuggets laid on the surface of the ground. It was Armstrong who discovered the deceased Hermit Wilson on Hermit Island in the 1850's.

In the 1940's a hermit, Martin Kane, lived on Oak Island living off the land and his skills. He produced maple sugar on the island, cut timber for a fishing boat, The Dreamer, and carried on such other commerce as a hermit could. In October of 1943, a fire broke out on the island, burning 4,000 acres over a period of many months while crews of firefighters attempted to extinguish smoldering duff and subsurface burn. During that same decade, a doctor from Illinois owned the island and decided to stock the island with goats and pigs. His attempt failed when bears and the severe winter killed off his stock.

In 1959, Oak Island became part of Apostle Islands State Forest. About that time, deer on Oak and many other islands were overpopulating, warranting a special long hunting season for herd management. Many sportsmen discovered the formidable terrain of Oak Island was more than they wanted to endure and decided it was one of the hunting grounds to avoid.

The island became part of the National Lakeshore in the early 1970's.

Moorage and Docking:

A little less than a mile and a half northwest of the sand spit, a National Park Service dock has been constructed. The dock has 80 feet of useable space on two sides, the shallower being the south side. Water depth at the outside end of the dock is 6-7 feet. Occasionally a sand bar forms 200 to 300 feet west of the dock and should be negotiated slowly by boats of more than 4 feet draft. This sand bottom shifts and changes over the winter and throughout the boating season. The bottom provides good anchorage under favorable wind conditions.

Boats can also anchor or beach along the other beaches on the island: one off the northwest corner of the island, two beaches between the clay banks on the north end and the rocky point at the northeast corner, one

Oak Island Dock.

small beach midway along the south side of the island, and off either side of the sand point at the southwest corner of the island. As in all cases, while approaching the beaches, boaters should watch for subsurface rocks.

Waters Surrounding the Island:

Water depths, east of the sand pint, are shallow along a shelf for most of the south side of Oak Island. West of the point, the water depths drop quickly although one encounters another shelf off the westernmost corner

Oak Island "Hole in the wall".

of the island. The remaining north and east coasts of the island, also, have sandstone and rock shelves. Depths drop more quickly on the south half of the east coast.

Along the 12 miles of Oak Island shoreline, pond nets are often placed midway between the southwest sand point and the dock, along the shore northwest of the dock, and off the sand beach of the northwest corner of the island. Gill nets are often found along the south shore of the island.

Fisheries:

From early spring to early summer, trolling for brown trout is good from the mainland shore to Oak Island and along the west shore of the island. As summer progresses, lake trout can be caught along Oak Island

and on the Oak Island Shoals north of the island.

Camping:

Campers should inquire at Park Headquarters for details on camping. Regularly scheduled shuttle boat service to Oak Island takes place throughout the season. Several campsites are available up the trail north of the dock. At the sand spit, several camps are located on the bank east of and above this point. Other locations are available for camping and can be identified by National Park personnel.

Hiking:

Presently, groomed and maintained trails lead from the dock to the clay banks at the north of the island and south along the shore to the sand point. This spectacular lookout shows a view of islands and "Hole-in-the-Wall" to the east. Trails being planned will extend to the northwest corner beach and also around the highest portion of the island. Park personnel can advise hikers of current trail conditions.

The Vicinity:

The mainland, including Frog Bay, lies between Red Cliff Point and Raspberry Point a mile west of Oak Island. To the northwest, two miles distant, is Raspberry Island. Bear Island can be seen two and a half miles north of Oak, with Devils Island seven and a half miles north. From the high clay banks, Otter, Rocky, Manitou, South Twin, Ironwood, North Twin, Cat and Outer Islands can be seen from two to 14 miles to the northeast. One and a half miles east of Oak lies Stockton Island. Southeast of Oak lies Hermit Island. Basswood Island lies three miles to the south. The West Channel originating in Chequamegon Bay, runs along the west coast of the island.

Rocks below the clay cliffs on Oak Island – east of Sand Spit – S.W.

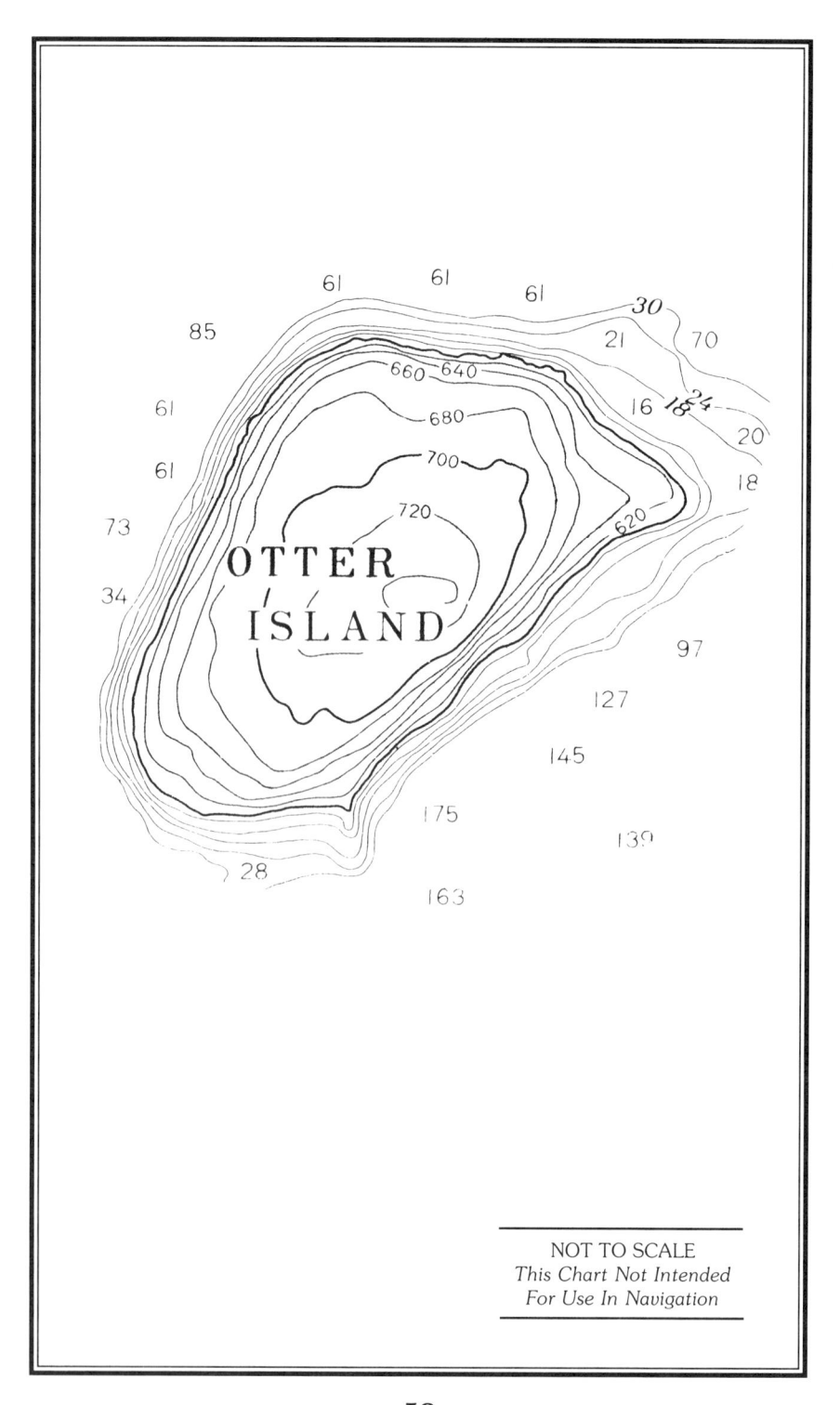

OTTER ISLAND

NOT TO SCALE
*This Chart Not Intended
For Use In Navigation*

Otter Island

Former Names:
Chippewa name – nigag miniss (Otter Island). Schoolcraft's name – Oregon. Former name – Alabama. Local name – Hardwood.

Size:
1,322 acres, about 2 miles long from southwest to northeast, $1^1/_4$ miles wide.

Characteristics of the Island:
Otter Island rises about 140 feet above lake level, with a gradual incline. The island is forested with hardwoods about 20 to 30 years of age. Tall rocky ledges are found along the north to northwest corners of the island. Most of the remainder of the circumference of the island slopes gradually to the shore. The southeast corner of the island ends in a sand point.

Historic Sites:
The most documented part of this island's history dates to June 1960, when 1,500 Boy Scouts and about 180 leaders overran the island on a Boy Scouts of America Camporee celebrating the merging of the Gitchee-

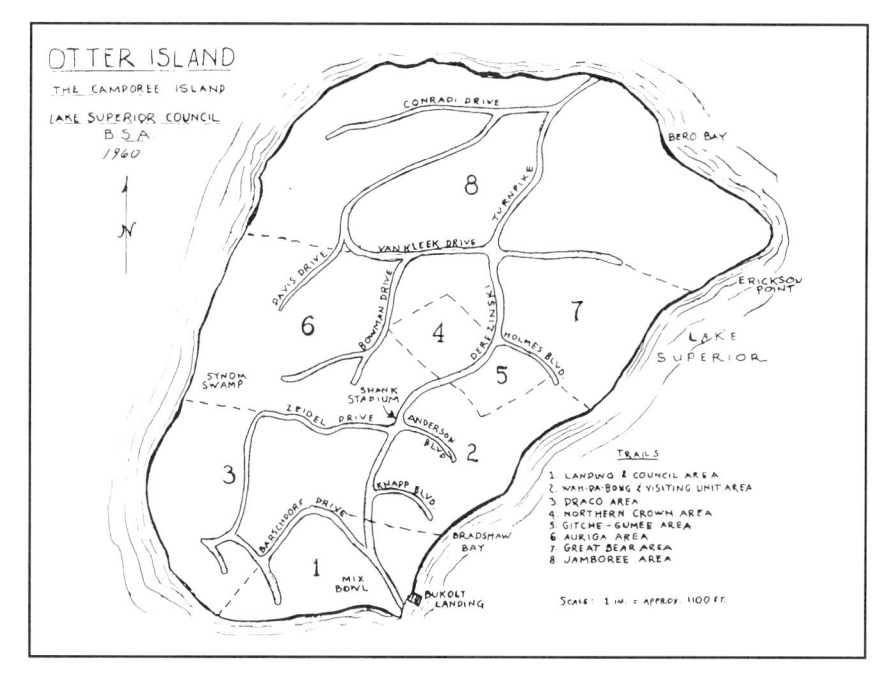

Gummee and North Star Councils into the new Lake Superior Council. They were transported in the Landing Craft OUTER ISLAND, in groups of 300. A number of area businesses and organizations donated materials, including a landing dock, to accommodate the Scouts. The Forest Service, ham radio operators, Coast Guard, Air National Guard, Air Force and other agencies joined to entertain and educate the Scouts. A map of the island shows trails and sections used for camping. Things have been considerably quieter on Otter Island since those early summer days in 1960.

A new dock replaced an old sunken barge. Depths are to seven feet.

Moorage and Docking:

An anchorage can be found on either side of the sand point at the southeast corner of the island. The former dock has been reconstructed and is a good landing.

Waters Surrounding the Island:

Beginning at the sand point and moving toward the northeast, one will find the depths dropping off gradually from the island. The northeast point of the island has a reef of rocks running a few hundred feet out. Off the remainder of the island, depths drop off consistently.

Winter transportation for ice fishermen.

Fisheries:

A trolling fishery for lake trout can be found on the Oak Island Shoal located about a mile southwest of the southwest corner of Otter Island.

Camping:

At present, there are facilities for campers on Otter Island. The forests have grown up from the time when the Camporee took place here, but a very good trail system can be found leading from the sand point to the northeast corner of the island.

The Vicinity:

Two miles south of Otter Island stands Oak Island, its tall clay cliffs and deep gulleys dropping down from 200 to 400 feet above the lake. At the northeast corner of Oak, one will find a sandstone wall with a hole eroded through it. To the southeast of Otter, one sees a small white box with a flashing white light perched atop a rock pile call Little Manitou. The Little Manitou light warns of the shoal extending below the surface between the light and Manitou Island east of it. Two miles east of Otter lies Ironwood Island, with Cat Island five miles distant in the same direction. South and North Twin Islands lie 2 and $5\frac{1}{2}$ miles respectively off to the northeast of Otter. North of Otter, less than a mile, is Rocky Island. North northwest 4 miles is Devils Island, the northernmost point of Wisconsin. Two miles to the west and northwest is Bear Island. Four miles southwest lies Raspberry Island, with the mainland shores near Raspberry Bay $5\frac{1}{2}$ miles from Otter.

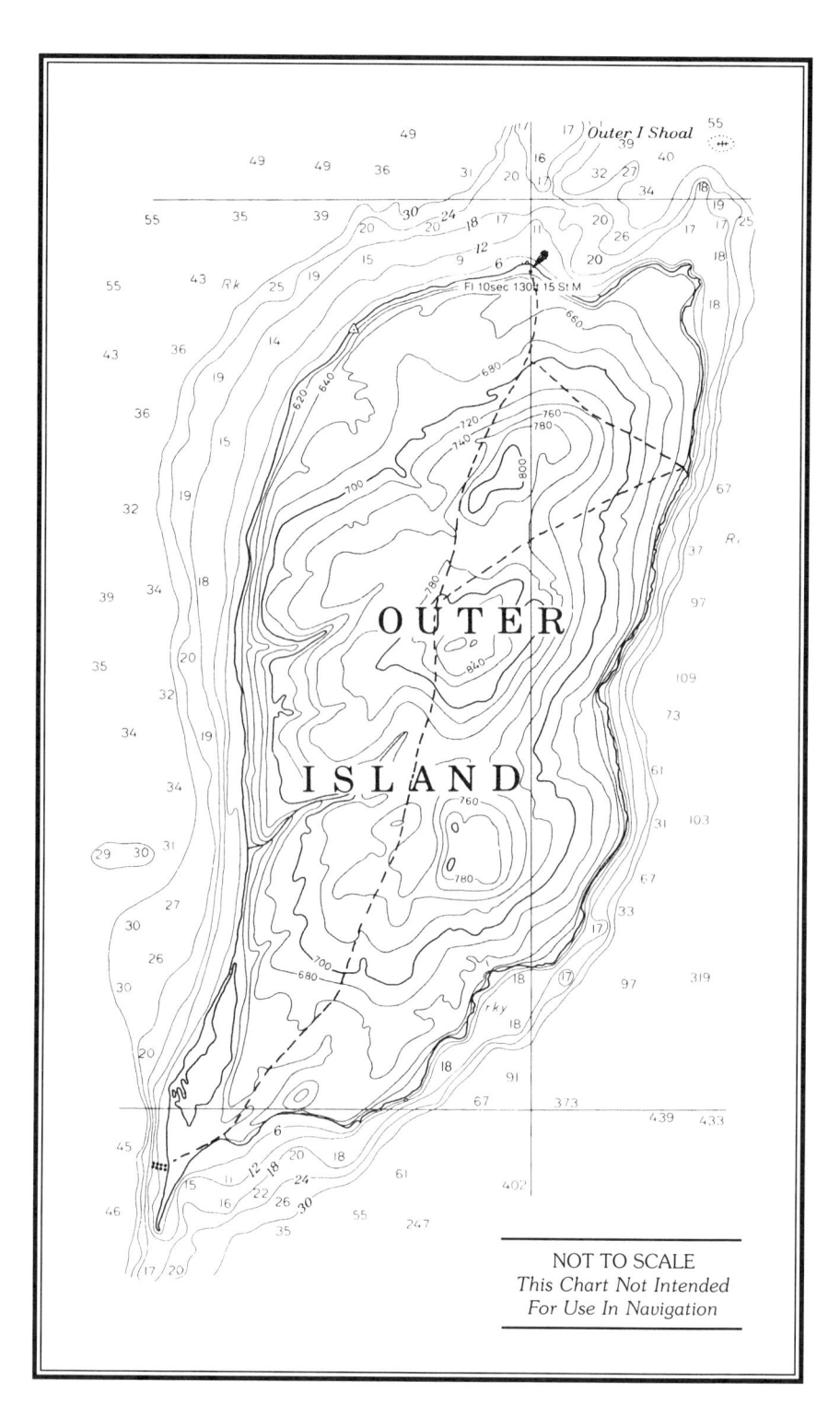

OUTER ISLAND

NOT TO SCALE
*This Chart Not Intended
For Use In Navigation*

Outer Island

Former Names:
Chippewa name – gachiishquaguindag miniss (Outermost Island). Schoolcraft's name – Ohio.

Size:
7,999 acres, $6\frac{1}{4}$ miles long, 2-$2\frac{1}{2}$ miles wide at the northern three-fourths of the island, tapering to a narrow sand point at the south end.

Characteristics of the Island:
Beginning at the south point, sand dunes from ten to 40 feet above water level extend a mile and three-quarters up the west side and about a mile up the east side. The sand creates a barrier for a lagoon from 3-8 feet deep which stretches about a mile north to south facing the clay banks that make up the major mass of the island. Clay overlays the remainder of the island preventing good drainage in the interior of the island. Deep drainage ravines are found along the west coast of the island. The northern two-thirds of the east coast of the island is rocky picturesque shoreline, laid bare by easterly storms. The southern third of this coast is clay banks, much like all of the west coast from the sand beach to the lighthouse at the north. A beach on the north end of the island from a rocky point to the lighthouse faces the magnificent expanse of Lake Superior.

Outer Island is forested with conifers on the sand at the south end to hardwoods and conifers of varying age and density throughout the rest of the island.

Outer Island dock and lighthouse. Northeast of the dock one mile lies the wreck of the Pretoria, 1905.

History:
In the early 1900's, Outer Island's shoals were the sites of groundings and disaster for several ships. The PRETORIA, a schooner

barge carrying $60,000 worth of iron ore, lost its rudder and was being towed by the tug VENEZUELA during the September 2, 1905, storm that sank the SEVONA off Sand Island earlier that day. The tow line snapped and the PRETORIA broke up on the shoals a mile northeast of the Outer Island Lighthouse. The VENEZUELA made it to the protected waters with all hands, but was unable to save the PRETORIA. In November of 1909, the STEAMER JAMES H. HOYT, 363 feet long, 3,934 tons, grounded two miles northeast of the island but was later pulled free. On September 4, 1914, the GEORGE H. VAN VLECK, burned near the island. In 1927, the steamer ONTARIO, 1,018 tons, foundered east of the island. Details of the ships lost without survivors are understandably vague, as Outer Island lies more than 25 miles from Bayfield.

Logging records indicate that white and red pines were cut off the island from 1900-1908. In 1922, the Schroeder Lumber Company began eight years of logging on the island. Their camp was established along a rail system centered about a third of the way up the island.
Miles of track was laid for two locomotives which railed the logs to the dock at the southwest side of the sand point. Hardwoods were barged to mills on the mainland. Hemlock and pine were floated in rafts towed by tugs. In 1926, the locomotives were no longer useful to the operation and were cut up for scrap at the dock. A coal tender remains beside the old railroad grade along with a company safe near the site of the Schroeder camp.

Slash from the logging operations burned on the island in 1930 and 1934, resulting in the aspen and white birch regrowth.

In the 1950's another logging operation began about a mile south of Austad Bay. This operation cut most of the north half of the island. Remnants of the camp include old cars and trucks, a sauna, cook shack, paymaster's shack, a pool table and a fancy 5-seat outhouse.

Another forest fire broke out because of lightning in 1963, burning about seven acres of forest on the island.

The lighthouse on the north end of Outer Island sends a beacon from 86 feet above the ground, 130 feet above the lake level, and is visible 15 miles. Its present Third Order electric lamp has a candlepower of 140,000 flashing white for 10 seconds. Its distinctive steam fog horn blasted until 1924. The light station is a complex of all-weather dock, a concrete walkway up the clay bank, the fog signal building, quarters attached to the white conical tower and sturdy brick outhouse. The view from the top of the light is panoramic, including most of Outer Island, islands to the west and south, the north shore of Lake Superior from Duluth-Superior to shore over 60 miles to the north.

Thanks to the U.S. Government lands around the lighthouse, virgin timber surrounds the area near the lighthouse.

Moorage and Docking:

The sole dock on Outer Island is the concrete dock at the lighthouse. Docking should be considered temporary and for small craft only. Large boulders are strewn on the bottom and there is often a surge in the seas coming off the open lake. The breakwall no longer serves the slip landward due to sediment. Up until 1967, a boathouse sheltered lightkeeper's boats. The boathouse was washed out during winter storms. The rocky bottom off the east 100 feet of the dock makes approach and docking risky in all except calm waters. The depth of the water at the outermost end of the dock is about five feet, shallowing toward shore. The safer approach is to

Outer Island Lighthouse, built in 1874, automated in 1961.

line up on the trainway from 100 yards out and to follow the straight and narrow path to the dock. Rocks are the hazard.

Temporary anchorage can be found along the stretch of beach east of the dock but should seldom be considered for long absences from the anchored vessel. *Large boulders lay all along the beach* beneath the surface.

East of the sand beach at the south sand point one can find a tentative anchorage. On the west side of the sand beach off the sand point, one will also find sand bottom for anchoring, though some of the bottom a mile north of the point is cobbles. Caution should be used approaching the old beached fishing boat three-quarters of a mile north of the point on the west side as subsurface pilings from the old dock still will be found.

Beaching a boat along any of the sand point beaches is easy though one should watch for cobbles when approaching the island.

Waters Surrounding the Island:

Shallow water extends several hundred yards south and east of the south tip of the sand point and this bottom also shifts east and west over time. For a mile and a half north of the point on the west coast of the island, the sand and cobble bottom drops off gradually. Care should be taken approaching the entire coast of clay bank on the west side as one will find, as in all approaches to clay banks, boulders in the banks mean boulders in the water. Boaters should take a wide berth around the northwest corner of the island all the way to the lighthouse due to a shallow shelf. Again, the approach to the lighthouse dock is strewn with boulders, as well as the approaches to the beach east of the lighthouse. At least two large vessels have grounded near the rocky ledges at the northeast point of the Island. These waters should be navigated with great caution, even though charts show depths up to 17 feet. A shelf runs out from Austad Bay and large boulders lie beneath the rocky cliffs along most of the east coast of the island, though water depths drop quickly. Along the southern third of the east coast, boulders continue. The boater should approach the southeast bay of the island cautiously due to the boulders. this is especially true beneath the clay banks. Most approaches to the east side of the sand point have a sand bottom that comes up gradually, except off the end of the sand point.

Pond nets are occasionally placed off the south end of the island and on the shoals west and midway up the island. Gill nets are occasionally placed off the west coast of the island.

Fisheries:

The Wisconsin Department of Natural Resources does not list any trolling opportunities off the coasts of Outer Island.

Camping:

Camping is allowed at different areas south of the lagoon area at the south end of the island. Current sites should be requested of the National Park Service at the headquarters. Outer Island camps have a magnificent aura of remoteness though boaters occasionally visit the sand point.

Hiking:

Trails were developed on Outer Island generally along the old railroad grade leading up the middle of the island. A trail can also be found leading from the lighthouse to Austad Bay. Outer Island is at its best for the beach hiker on the west coast where one can often find beach to walk on one-third of the way along the west shore. Hiking along the north two-thirds of

Beachcombers on one of the Apostle Islands.

the east coast of the island is also special, though the hiker will often encounter places where rock cliffs and the tangle of tenacious foliage will seem to be conspiring against human intrusion.

The Vicinity:

As the name indicates, Outer Island is the outermost island. Open Lake Superior will be found east and north of the island. The north end of Outer is very much in line with the north ends of North Twin and Devils Island 8 and 15 miles westward. Cat Island is found four miles west of the middle of Outer. Stockton lies southwest of Outer Island three miles. Michigan and Gull Islands can be seen about seven miles south of Outer Island. when looking from the south shore of Outer Island on a clear day, one sees the south shore of Lake Superior extending from about the Michigan/Wisconsin state lines eastward along the rolling hills of the Gogebic Range, the Porcupine Mountains and the Keweenaw Peninsula which fades into the lake toward the east. On those clear days, one can sometimes pick out the 600-foot scaffold of the Copper Peak Ski Flying Jump near Black River Harbor, Michigan, 40 miles distant.

The Apostle Islands are nesting sites for a great variety of birds.

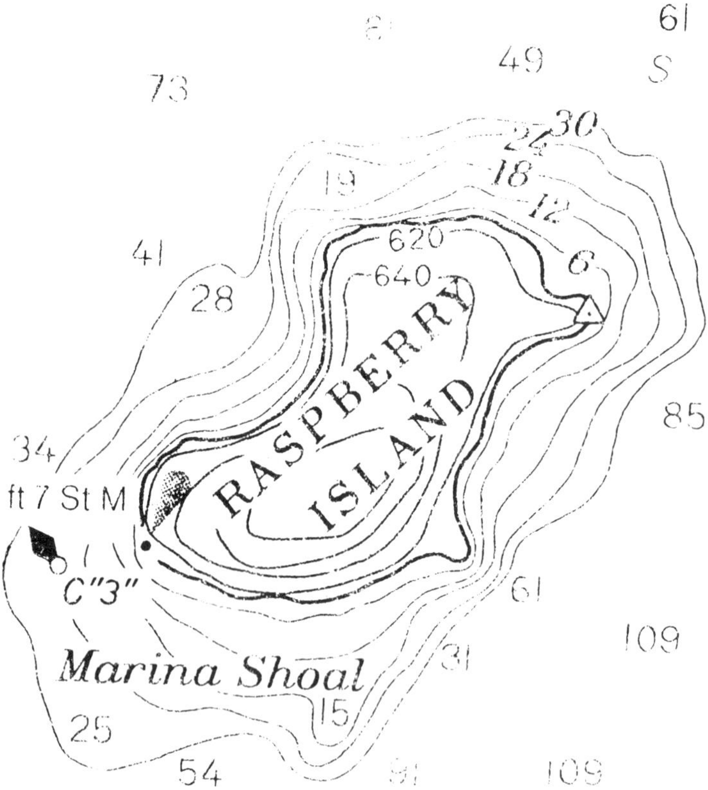

NOT TO SCALE
This Chart Not Intended
For Use In Navigation

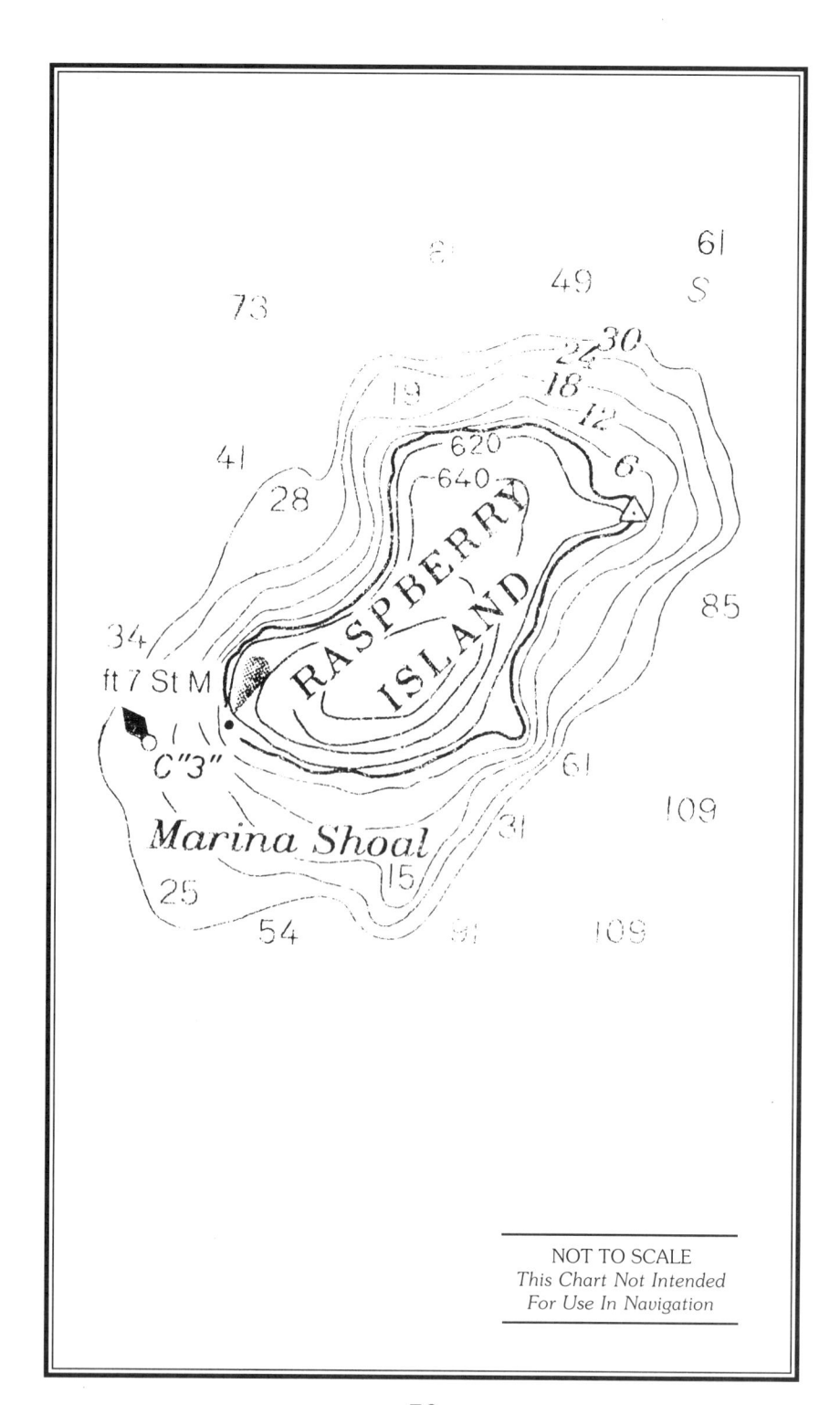

Raspberry Island

Former Name:
Chippewa – miskominikan miniss (Island of Raspberries).

Size:
Raspberry Island is about $1/2$ mile wide, 1 mile long, 296 acres.

Historic Sites:
Raspberry Island is the site of the second lightstation built among the islands. Its present automated light marks the west channel. The light, first operated during the 1864 navigation season, was later to include a double dwelling for keepers and families. According to letters and journals written during the days of manned light stations, lightkeepers' families competed with one another for productive and beautiful gardens. The Raspberry Lighthouse flower gardens were acknowledged as being the most beautiful as they framed the large white duplex. At the present time, the light station is occupied by a park ranger. The National Park Service is considering refurnishing the lighthouse with some of the original furnishings and has replanted gardens to return the lighthouse to its former splendor.

Visits to the lighthouse are possible when the ranger is on duty. An excursion boat lays over on the island frequently during the summer for visitors wishing to enter the lighthouse and walk the $1/2$ mile to the scenic sand point at the southeast end of the island.

Docking and Anchorages:
Raspberry Island has one of the favorite anchorages among the islands. The southeast corner of the island offers good protection on either side of the sand point. It has a good sand bottom and the scenery is idyllic. Docking can be found at the southwest corner of the island below the lightstation. Here the short dock offers six feet of less water depth on the outside, four feet or less on the inside. Approaches should be away

Raspberry Island Lighthouse can be seen on guided tours. The Park Service plans to restore the light station even more.

from the shore south of the dock as large boulders from the eroding clay cliffs are strewn about near the shore. Vessels passing from the dock to the sand point should be aware of the marina shoal a few hundred yards south of the dock and west of the sand point. Check a navigation chart. There is occasionally a pond net located at that marina shoal.

Waters Surrounding the Island:

Other than the boulders located south of the dock and the marina shoal, and the pond net off the southwest corner of the island, the depths around the rest of the island drop off gradually without unusual hazards. An abrupt dropoff is located south off the sand point.

Fishing:

A trolling area is located east of Raspberry on the Oak Island shoal. Another can be found on the York Island shoal northeast of Raspberry Island.

Hiking and Camping:

Camping is presently not allowed on the island. A hiking trail connects the sandspit with the lighthouse complex.

The Vicinity:

Raspberry Island 5th order Fresnel Lens, installed 1891 with flash panels to produce a bright flash every 90 seconds. Can be seen at the Madeline Island Museum.

One of the most appealing scenes anywhere among the islands can be seen from the Raspberry Lighthouse. Westward one sees the green forested islands, York and Sand. North of Raspberry Island, about 35 miles, is Taconite Harbor, where one occasionally sees the radar towers and the rolling hills of the Minnesota North Shore. Northwest is Silver Bay. It is not unusual to see an ore boat or freighter somewhere along the shipping channels in the distance to the west or north. Bear Island rises about a mile and a half northeast of Raspberry. Otter Island is east three miles. Oak Island, with its 200 foot tall clay cliffs, faces Raspberry to the southeast. To the southwest $1\frac{1}{2}$ miles, on the mainland, is Raspberry Bay.

Raspberry Island Lighthouse, built in 1863 to mark the west channel, is open to visitors.

Photo by Claire Duquette

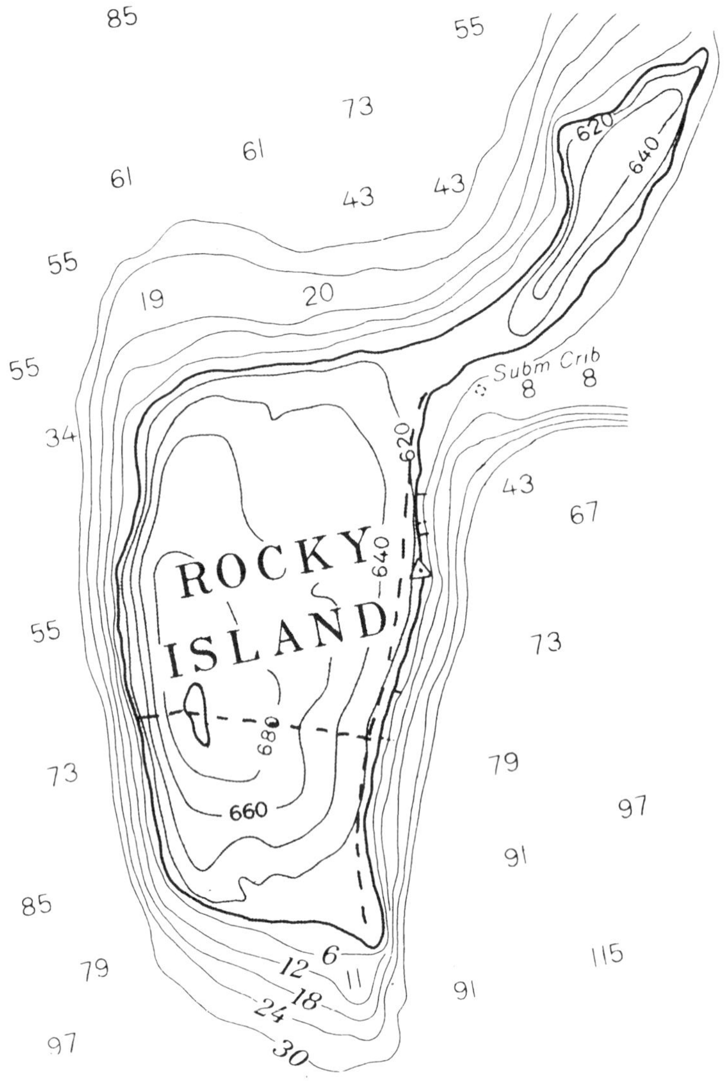

NOT TO SCALE
This Chart Not Intended
For Use In Navigation

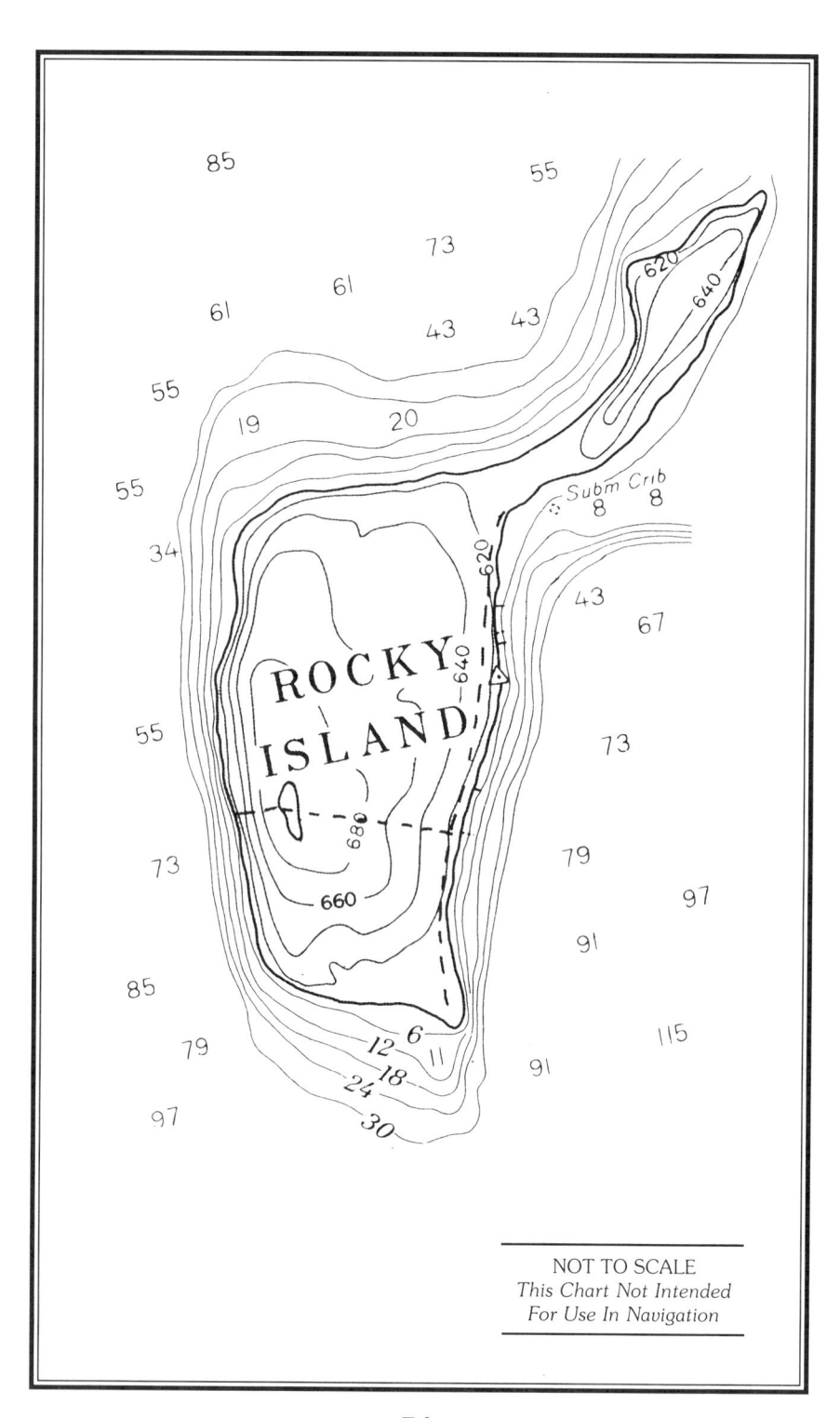

Rocky Island

Former Names:
Chippewa name – sinsibakawado miniss (Maple Sugar Island). Schoolcraft's name – Mississippi. Local name – Rice's.

Size:
1,099 acres, about 2 miles long, northeast to southwest. The lower half of the island is about a mile wide; the upper portion extends like a goose-neck a couple hundred yards wide.

Characteristics of the Island:
Much of the shoreline on the southern part of the island is lined with rocks, hence, the name. Sand beaches can also be found at the south end, along most of the east side and on the northwest side. Clay cliffs line the west part of the southern portion. Clay cliffs also line the northern tip of the island.

Several buildings can be found on Rocky Island from the south tip to the north tip.

A National Park Service Ranger is usually on duty here.

Moorage and Docking:

The National Park dock is the southernmost dock on the island. It is located on the east side, identifiable by the National Park Service sign on shore. There is often considerable competition for dock space here. Boats must be docked stern or bow to the dock. Depths at the dock are down to 12 feet at the outside end of the dock, shallowing toward shore. Mooring is secure except in northeast or southeast winds. Anchorages are in a sand bottom.

Waters Surrounding the Island:

The best guide for determining water conditions around Rocky Island is the navigation chart. Special caution should be taken by boaters off the north tip of the island where large boulders lie in the water near the eroding shore.

Fishing Opportunities:

Most trolling is done near Devils and North Twin Islands rather than near Rocky Island.

Camping and Hiking:

Trails on public lands lead through the south half of the island. A trail map is posted near the National Park Service dock. Seven camp sites are also marked and campers must use established sites.

The Vicinity:

East of Rocky Island lies South Twin. South lies Otter Island. West is Bear Island. Northwest lies Devils Island.

Snowshoeing, skiing and winter camping can be enjoyed in the Apostle Islands National Lakeshore.

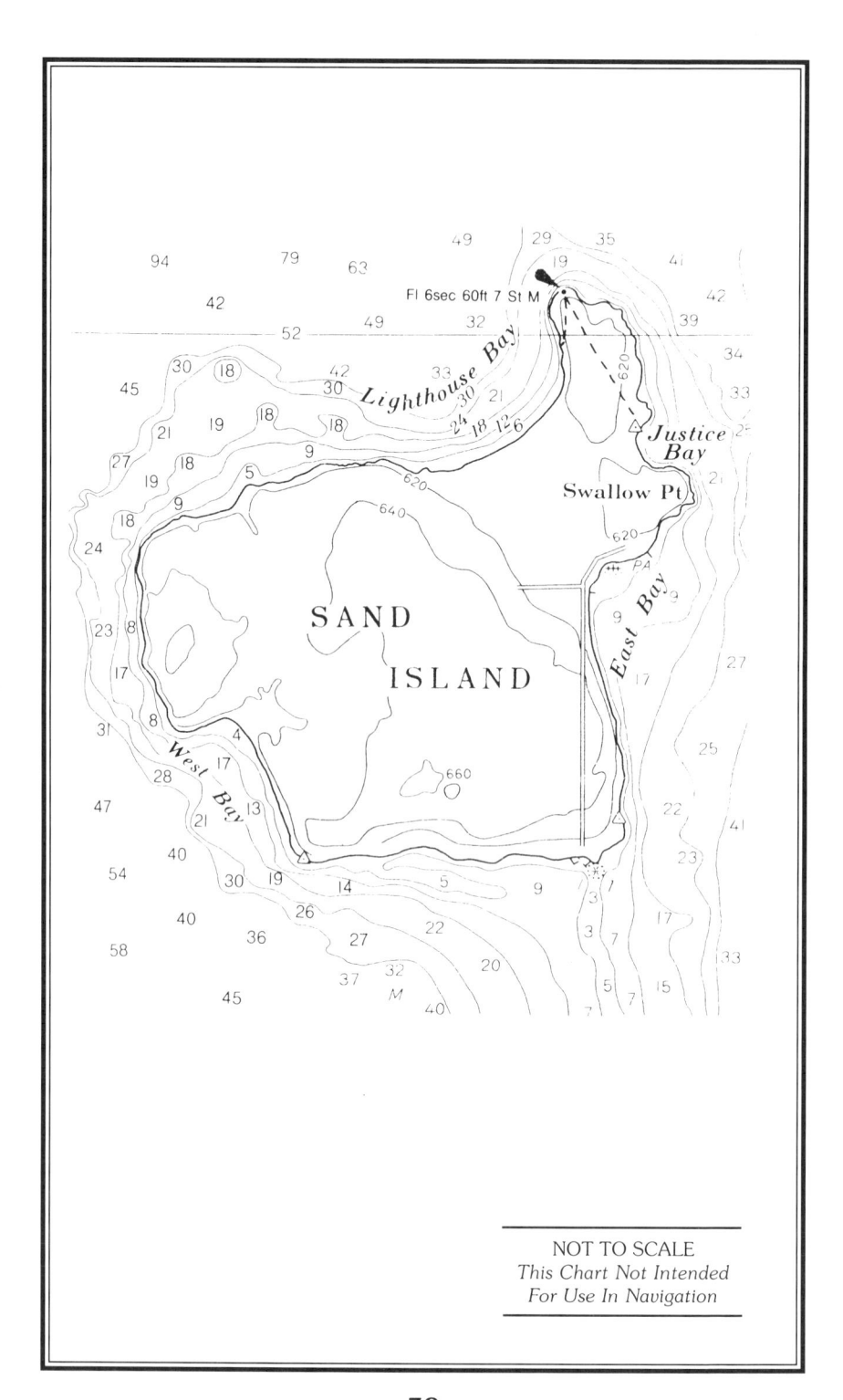

NOT TO SCALE
*This Chart Not Intended
For Use In Navigation*

Sand Island

Former Names:
Chippewa name – wababiko miniss (White Rock Island). Schoolcraft's name – Massachusetts.

Size:
2,949 acres.

Characteristics of the Island:
Sand Island is a flat wet island, rising 50 feet above the lake level at its highest. The interior, as a result, has poor drainage and extensive wet areas.

Its tenacious vegetation has reclaimed the land. Clay overlays the sandstone base of the island. The trees are a mixture of conifers and hardwoods. Underbrush is usually berries and American yew or ground hemlock which grows in such profusion that one can find yew branches towering over one's head. "Old Man's Beard" hangs in scraggly goatees from the branches of the conifers along the north shore of the island. Those willing to brave the vegetation will often be treated with unusual beauty along the way – lady's slipper orchids, colorful mushrooms, moss beds rivaling the most lush carpets, sprays of shadow and sunshine seldom experienced where the land has been tamed.

A sailboat and dingy, the means of landing on the more remote islands.

Historic Sketch:

Two islands among the Apostles were the sites of villages, La Pointe on Madeline Island and Shaw on Sand Island. Shaw was named after the island's first resident. The small community was make up of fishermen and their families. Over the years the village eventually developed a post office, school, grocery store, linked together by a telephone system. A road ran the length of the village and extended to the lighthouse. This proud little village dissolved when the fishing industry began its decline, when self-sustaining farming provided too meager an existence, and when a pioneer period came to an end. At present one will find landmarks of the island's

In direct response to growing traffic at the west end of Lake Superior, Sand Island Light was built in 1881. Theh native brownstone of the Sand Island LIght makes it one of the most picturesque of the lighthouses of the Great Lakes.

Photo by Claire Duquette

former lifestyle.

At the north end of the island, one finds perhaps, the most beautiful lighthouse among the islands. Its hard oil lamp was lighted for the first time on a September night in 1881. The lighthouse is constructed of native sandstone with a Gothic Revival appearance. The lightkeeper, in September, 1905, helplessly watched the 3,100-ton steamer SEVONA break up in 25-35 foot waves a mile and a half northeast of the light. Following the wreck, he and the residents of Shaw rescued survivors and retrieved the dead along the Sand Island beaches, at Justice and East Bays.

A logging camp is located in West Bay where a timber lodge once housed the loggers. In those days, the men used a grass landing strip north of East Bay for aircraft to fly in their supplies.

Hiking and Camping:

Camping off the end of the East Bay Dock is popular for groups and individuals. A very good trail runs from the dock to the lighthouse at the north end of the island, much of it boardwalk.

Sand Island winter with Lightkeeper Luick in the early winter.. NPS photo

Moorage and Docking:

A National Park Service wooden dock for public use is located near the inside corner of East Bay. Docking is available on both sides for about 80 feet of the dock, depending on the delta found at the end of a drainage. Potable well water is available west of the dock.

East Bay offers a good anchorage. This bottom is mostly sand.

Justice Bay is a picturesque cove at the northeast corner of Sand Island. The sand cliffs of Swallow Point and the small beach make this bay one of the most beautiful among the islands. The bottom is mostly sand, with cobbles near the north shore of the cove and fallen pieces of sandstone along the south shore.

At the North point of Sand Island, at the lighthouse, a sandstone ledge below the lighthouse is only approachable under conditions of almost perfect calm. Beware of subsurface rocks.

At Lighthouse Bay a sand bottom runs far out to the north, allowing anchorage under proper wind conditions. The beach is not very deep but extends a long ways west to east. Rocks will be found in the water, naturally, off the rocky shores of the bay. Watch for north, northwest and northeast storms at this anchorage.

On the northwest side, although sandstone ledges might be landings, extreme caution should be exercised, for reefs run out a long distance.

West Bay has an anchorage with a sand bottom. Be aware of rocks west of the drainage 100 feet from shore and rocks along the north shore.

Waters Surrounding the Island:

South of Sand Island lies a sand bar that extends from the island to the mainland shore. Depths vary from less than 5 to 30 feet or more. A bow lookout and sounder are advised. The bottom changes. A chart gives only a general idea of the depths here. Passage is possible for shallow draft boats but should be done nearer the island than the mainland.

Boating near the southeast corner of the island requires caution, as the bottom is generally rocky near shore.

East Bay is fairly uniform in depth but the sand bottom turns to rock a little north of the main National Park Service dock, almost straight east to a shoal extending southeast from Swallow Point. Depths drop off abruptly off Swallow Point, though one must watch for the large fallen rocks below the cliffs. Justice Bay has good depth in the center of the bay. The shoreline on the northeast corner of the island is best avoided as shoals skirt this point out to the lighthouse. Ledges off the lighthouse are often fronted by fallen rocks. Caution and a lookout are a must all along this point from the light to the beach westward in Lighthouse Bay. Again, west of the bay, rock shoals extend out from the shoreline and approaches to the island here should be extremely cautious. One might approach a small beach west of the northwest corner of the island in a small boat. The northwest corner of the island to West Bay lies below rocky ledges where caution should be taken and the bottom watched as one moves slowly southward.

West Bay offers a good water depth in the center, with rocks along the north and east shores. A boulder lies just below the surface 100 feet west of the drainage at the east side of the bay. Boaters should be aware of several other submerged boulders within the bay. Along the west shore, one finds clay banks with occasional boulders in the water near shore. The southwest corner of the island occasionally is the site of a pond net. The south shore of the island varies between rocky to sandy and it is generally advisable to cruise out 100 yards or more. An old fisherman and former resident of the island who knew each rock and shoal, advised that you "Hold away from Sand Island unless you know where the hard spots are."

The Vicinity:

South of Sand Island lies the mainland across a little more than a mile and a half of shallow sand bar. The Sand River enters the lake south of the island. Southeast of the island lies Little Sand Bay, a National Lakeshore dock and information facility, and the Hokenson Fisheries dock which will remain a landmark of the earlier fishing days. York Island is the closest island to the east of Sand. Northeast of Justice Bay lies the Sand Island shoals, site of the SEVONA wreck. About six miles north of the island are the shipping channels where one will often see oreships and freighters plying westward to the Twin Ports of Superior-Duluth, eastbound to Sault Ste. Marie, the lower great lakes and the world. Beyond the shipping lanes one sees the north shore near Silver Bay and Taconite Harbor, two shipping ports for the Iron Range of Minnesota. West of Sand Island about 55 miles is Superior-Duluth. Eagle Island and the Squaw Bay sea caves lie three and four miles respectively southwest of Sand Island.

Fishery:

Lake trout and brown trout can be trolled for at the mouth of the Sand River and on the north and west sides of Sand Island.

NOT TO SCALE
*This Chart Not Intended
For Use In Navigation*

84

Stockton Island

Former Names:

Chippewa name – gegawewamingo miniss (Burnt Wood Island), also genawewauindag miniss (Almost an Island). French name – Presqu'ile or Presque Isle (Almost an Island). Schoolcraft's name – Pennsylvania. Local name – Presque Isle.

Stockton was the name of a mapmaker who obviously wanted his name on the island.

Size:

10,054 acres, 7¼ miles east of west, 2-2½ miles wide; second largest of the Apostle Islands.

Historic Sites:

Because of its size and nearness to Madeline Island, Stockton Island's popularity as a seasonal camp extends back as far as 3,000 years or more. Artifacts from Early Woodland Indians have been found on the island, suggesting that these early campers found the island as good a campsite as present day campers. More recent visitors have spent time on the island harvesting blueberries, fishing and hunting. Fire scars on trees in the Julian Bay Lagoon portion of the island reveal that berry pickers practiced principles of "land management" using fire to burn off older blueberry bushes to rejuvenate the plants and improve the harvest. These controlled fires were used as recently as the 1970's.

Stockton Island – Presqu'ile main dock.

Parts of Stockton Island were logged during the 1870's and the practice continued on some portions of the island until the 1940's. A shack used by one recent logging camp can be found beside a ravine at the southwest corner of Stockton. Camps were also located along the north coast of the island and at the north end of the tombolo that makes Presqu'ile Point.

Proposed uses of the island at about the time of World War I included a plan to utilize the island as a holding area for beef cattle which were being shipped from the West to the markets in the East. Cattle would be boated from the railheads to the islands, held until the market demanded, and than shipped by boat and rail to large city markets. One proposal called for 1,500 steers and 5,000 hogs to be detained on the island, but the plan never went into effect. A proposal was also made to create a boys camp on the island, but their association with the steers and hogs is not clear.

Fish camps were established on Stockton Island and were used until the decline of the trout populations in the 1950's. Clearings and occasional remnants of docks indicate the general locations at Trout Point, the north end of Julian Bay, near the dock on Presqu'ile, in the clearing northwest of the Presqu'ile dock, and at Quarry Bay. These camps usually consisted of living quarters, net and equipment sheds, and ice sheds. The remains of a fish camp on Manitou Island suggests the general make-up of the fish camps. These camps were served by the Booth Fishery's collection boat which would alternately stop at a specific group of islands on a particular day of the week. When the collection boat stopped at Manitou Island, for example, it would also stop at Madeline, Sand, and Bear Islands that day.

Researchers draw data and tag black bears on Stockton Island, site of a large population of black bears.

Quarry Bay was named for its proximity to a sandstone quarry which operated a little more than a mile west of Quarry Bay. At present, a trail leads to the quarry site, a huge excavation whose opening to the shore is a narrow cut where sandstone blocks were moved by rails to the barges for transport to railheads. This quarry was the largest of the island quarries and, like the others, discontinued operations in the early 1900's.

In 1959, Stockton Island became part of the Apostle Islands State Forest, along with Oak Island and part of Basswood Island. Camping by modern campers began to increase at that time. In 1975, the islands in the State Forest were transferred to Apostle Islands National Lakeshore.

Moorage and Docking:

The most substantial dock on Stockton Island is located on the west side of Presque Isle Point. It is a concrete dock, 250 feet long, with about 160 feet of the landward side useable for docking. Part of the dock is reserved for the Park Ranger's boat. Another dock extends from the shore north of the concrete dock, enclosing a marina. Since this dock is very pop-

Stockton Island dock is a popular overnight and day use site.

ular, time limit regulations allow for a variety of uses, i.e., off-loading by the Excursion shuttle, short-term docking and overnight docking.

Water depths vary, the deepest being 7 feet of water at the end of the dock. Boats approaching the dock should be aware that the rock rubble mound protects the outside cell of the dock and the rocks extend a short distance below the surface from the cell. Rubble also protects the outside of the dock and this side is not useable for docking. Boaters should also be aware that the space between the dock and shore is not dredged and that sand bars shift near shore. A recurrent problem boaters have is watching for dock space while ignoring the depths near shore. A new dock runs perpendicular to shore towards the end of the main dock. Boats must dock either stern or bow to the dock to allow more boats to use the space available. A resident National Park Service Ranger can advise boaters of effective use of the dock, and point out what to see and do on the island.

An excellent anchorage can be found all along the west side of Presque Isle Bay. The depths are uniform and the bottom is sand.

A picturesque but tentative anchorage will be found on the east side of Presque Isle Point and Julian Bay. The bottom is sand except at the extremities of the bay. This anchorage is exposed to open lake toward the east and has been the site of middle-of-the-night scrambles and groundings when the wind shifted and skippers slept too well.

Quarry Bay has a wood dock 95 feet long, with about 70 useable feet on both sides. It is typically shallow with about 4 feet of water at the outside end.

A very good anchorage can be found within Quarry Bay. The bottom is sand. While placing an anchor, one should be cautious of the weeds in some parts of the bay which might foul the anchor.

One might anchor briefly off the northwest beach of Stockton Island for beachcombing. A sand bottom along most of the north end of the island allows temporary anchorage for boaters.

Waters Surrounding the Island:

Along the 23-mile shoreline of Stockton Island, the boater will find a variety of water conditions. As in all approaches to the islands, a watch should be placed on the bow when nearing the island.

The waters near the Presque Isle dock are generally a consistent depth 100 yards or more from the shore. A notable hazard in the water is an old crib about 100 feet from shore northeast of the outside cell of the concrete dock. As one moves northwest in the bay, depth get shallower farther and farther from shore. A trap net is occasionally set off the northernmost part of the bay. One should avoid these nets and all net markers unless one knows a great deal about them.

Between Presque Isle Bay and Quarry Bay one will find rocks and sand along the shore and should exercise caution if cruising in close. Depths in Quarry Bay are generally good. West of Quarry Bay one finds the depths dropping off from the rocky shore quite abruptly – to over 200 feet within a hundred yards of the shoreline. As one cruises along the west side, the bottom drops down more gradually. From the beach at the northwest corner of Stockton to the north end of Trout Point, one finds a shelf off the island, usually a sand bottom mixed with occasional rocks. From

Ice fishing among the islands for trout and herring.

Trout Point to the far east point of Stockton, one finds tumbled down rocks in the water along the shore. South of eastmost point and all along this side, to Julian Bay, one finds large slabs of sandstone in the water. Balancing Rock projects out of a small bay. Water depths around the rock area are from 4 to 7 feet and a small craft can circumnavigate the rock. A

A Stockton Island beachcomber.

little farther south, a smaller standing rock will be found. This one is in shallow water. One should not cruise too close to shore along this side as large boulders line the shore. Around the point leading into the north end of Julian Bay, one will find a variety of boulders extending out from shore, generally to be avoided by the casual boater. The sand bottom of Julian Bay varies in depth near shore, being most irregular near the mouth of the intermittent stream that drains the lagoon area behind the dunes. As one nears the south end of the bay, one again finds rocks in the water beneath the rocky shoreline. From this point on, all the way around Anderson Point, boaters should hold well away from shore as the rock shelf extends out 100 yards or more in places. South of the east side of Anderson Point, a large subsurface rock is located 50 yards or more from shore. A pond net is often placed off the west tip of Anderson Point. Depths from the point to the Presque Isle dock drop gradually from the shore.

Once again, there is a great variety in the 23-mile shoreline of

Stockton Island. These cursory outlines of "Waters Surrounding the Island" are intended to warn boaters away from danger points and are never intended to guarantee the absence of subsurface hazards. All shorelines unknown to the boater should be approached in direct proportion to the value one places on himself and his vessel.

Camping:

Stockton Island is the favorite camping island among the Apostle Islands for at least three good reasons: it is large, accessible, and has some of the most attractive features found on any of the islands. The camping possibilities vary from maintained, well-placed sites for individuals and family groups, to larger group sites, and to back country sites.

Beginning at the dock, 20 individual and family sites are located along the arching beach of Presque Isle Bay. A trail leads from the dock/ranger station area to the camp sites. Well water is available at the head of the dock with pit toilets, information boards, picnic area and Park Naturalist's campfire circle nearby. Each campsite has a fire place and a designated location for tent(s). All sites are visually separated from each other and each has a view of Presque Isle Bay. Sites are available on a first-come basis with a two week use limit. In the 1990's a fee is charged.

Group camp sites are located at Quarry Bay. These are specifically designed to accommodate groups of ten or more. As groups may not use family sites in Presque Isle Bay, advance arrangements should be made with the National Park Service for use of the group sites.

Back country sites are scattered along trails and in some clearings away from the two maintained camping areas. Arrangements should be made and information exchanged with the resident Ranger for a Back Country Camping Permit.

Long sandy beaches for swimming and beachcombing, secluded campsites, beautiful vistas, shoreline trails, wildlife and unusual features, such as the bog and lagoon area, can be found on Stockton Island.

Hiking:

Trails originate at the Presque Isle dock and where the trailhead map shows the loop trail around Anderson Point. This loop trail leads through a cliff and forest environment. One will find secluded shoreline vistas across the channel to Michigan, Gull and Madeline Islands, rocky shelves running into the lake, "Singing Sands" beach, and the bog and lagoon overlook along this two mile trail.

For hikers wishing to go only a short distance, the $1/2$ mile hike across the point to Julian Bay is a must. When easterly winds blow, surf rolling into the beach roars and crashes on the beautiful mile and a quarter of sand. Beneath a warm sun, it is hard to envision a more beautiful paradise. Picnic tables are placed along the dunes between the lakeshore and the lagoon inland. A walk back to the lagoon and bog area will sometimes turn up a sand hill crane, ducks, blackbirds, and even geese. The pines here show fire scars that may have resulted from times when berry pickers would burn off old bushes to improve the blueberry patches. The berries yield plentifully in later July and early August. A look into the lagoon at different points might reveal the trail of a clam, a wiggle of pollywogs, a few evasive frogs and schools of minnows. Occasionally hikers report seeing a pike or panfish drifting in the landlocked water.

At the edge of the bog is a variety of plant succession communities where swamp grasses, pitcher plants and low bog brush guard the shoreline. This area is part of a sand bar that developed between the rock island which is now Anderson Point and the main island which rises north of the lagoon/bog area. This joining barrier is called a "tombolo" by geologists. It is over 6,000 years old and from an airplane one can clearly see the succession of beaches which have developed between the two former islands.

The Vicinity:

Stockton Island's Presqu'ile dock is located 15 miles from Bayfield. The southwest corner of the island is about two miles north of the east end of Madeline. Hermit Island can be seen southwest of Stockton's southeast corner. Oak Island if found one and a half miles west of Stockton, with Manitou, Ironwood and Cat Islands lying about two miles north of the north coast of Stockton. The south end of Outer lies in a northeasterly direction three miles from Trout Point. Michigan Island lies across a deep channel southeast of Presqu'ile Point (Anderson Point).

Fisheries:

Pond nets, trap nets and gill nets can be found at different points all around Stockton Island. On the south side, a pond net is often found to the west of Anderson Point, and a trap net is occasionally placed inside Presqu'ile Bay. Gill nets can often be seen off the southeast corner of the island and along the west coast. Along the north coast, a pond net will often be placed a third of the way eastward from the northeast corner of the island with gill nets along the way out to Trout Point. Along the west side of the island, a gill net is occasionally placed east of Julian Bay. Winter bobbing is relatively popular for lake trout off the southwest and south corners of Stockton during February when fishermen can sometimes be found near the edges of the ice shelf before the ice is continuous to the island.

A pond or pound net for fishing Whitefish.

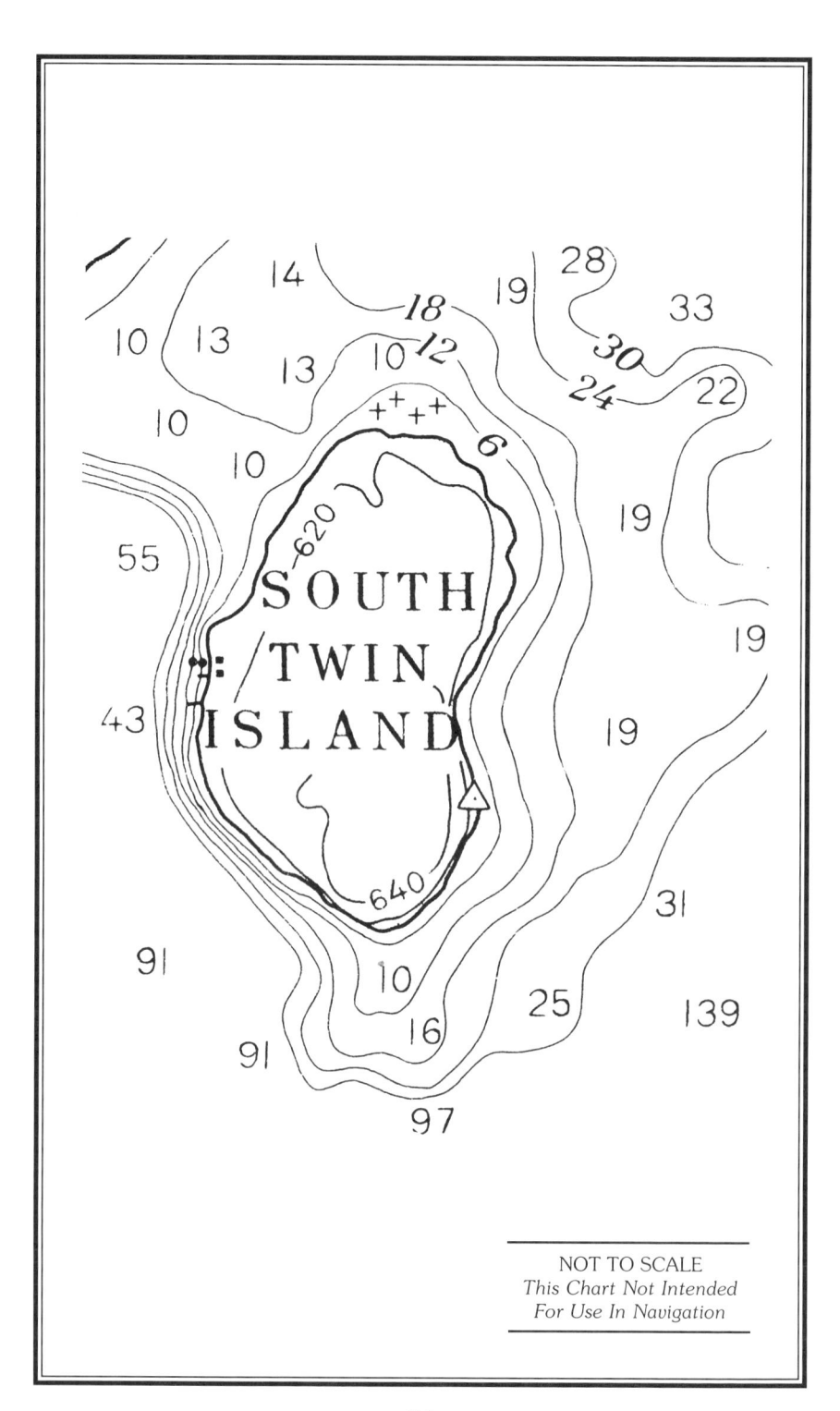

NOT TO SCALE
This Chart Not Intended For Use In Navigation

South Twin Island

Former Names:
Chippewa name – wasabo miniss (Rabbit Island). Schoolcraft's name – Georgia. Local name – Willey's. Former name – Shoal.

Size:
360 acres, about a mile long, three-quarters mile wide.

Characteristics of the Island:
South Twin is the only island in the National Lakeshore which has no rock outcroppings as part of its shoreline.

Along the west central shore of the island, a clearing with two buildings marks the site of present Ranger residences and former fish camp buildings or private cabins. South of the cabins one can see a long clearing which used to be an airstrip for the former island owner.

Docking and Mooring:
South Twin has a dock on the west central side with deep water. (See "Docks.") Sand makes up most of the bottom between Rocky and South Twin Island, so good anchorages might be found in the vicinity of the docks. A boardwalk leads to an information and display area.

Waters Surrounding the Island:
The north shore of the island is bordered with rocks in shallow water. Water depth is irregular around South Twin; pay close attention to the chart. One of the most obvious bottom conditions around South Twin is the sand bar extending between Rocky and South Twin. Depths vary from year to year.

A pond net is often placed off the southwest shore of South Twin.

Camping and Hiking:
Camping is permitted on South Twin Island. Designated campsites can be pointed out by the ranger on Rocky or South Twin.

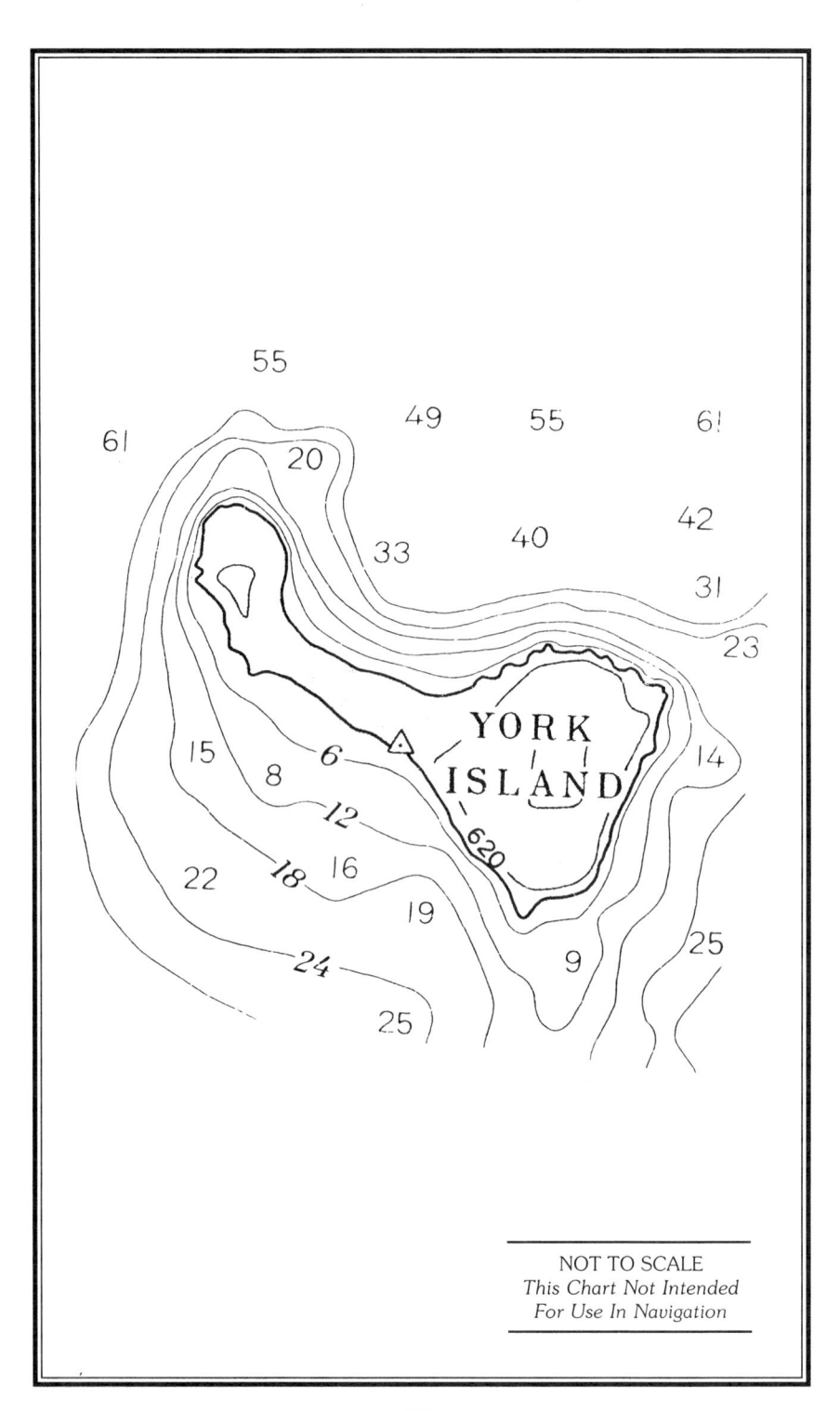

YORK ISLAND

NOT TO SCALE
*This Chart Not Intended
For Use In Navigation*

96

York Island

Former Names:
Chippewa name – miskwabimijikag miniss (Willow Tree Island). Schoolcraft's name – Connecticut.

Size:
320 acres; a narrow mile-long section about 150 yards wide at the northwest, ending in a portion about $1/2$ mile wide at the southeast end.

Characteristics of the Island:
A survey done by the British naval lieutenant Henry W. Bayfield in 1824 shows two islands, the eastern one called York, the western called Rock. There were later joined by a sand bar, as they are today.

At present, the narrow northwest third of the island is sandstone covered with a tangle of trees. The middle third of the island is the sand bar 100 to 150 yards wide, creating a long sweeping beach, with the majority of trees on the south side and the majority of beach on the north side. The southeast third of the island is relatively flat sandstone covered by a weatherbeaten entanglement of trees. The southwest portion of the island ends in a sand point.

Moorage and Docking:
There are no docks on York Island, but a tentative landing can be found off the rock ledges at the northeast end of the island. Far better are the anchorages which present themselves north of the beach – but – as in all cases where one is exposed to open lake, the boater should keep a wary eye on wind and weather changes. One can beach shallow draft boats along the beach but should be cautious of submerged rocks at either end of the extreme ends of the beach. Near the sand point at the south end of the island, one might also beach or anchor close to the west side. Once again, the boater should post a watch for submerged rocks when approaching the island.

Waters Surrounding the Island:
After referring to the navigation chart, the boater should be aware of these hazards: south of the northwest arm of the island – a long way from shore – are submerged boulders. Any approach to the northern two-thirds of the island from the south should be cautious. Southeast of the sand point and all along the southeast portion of the island within a couple hundred yards, approaches should be cautious. Here, the clay cliffs have gradually

eroded leaving boulders in the relatively shallow water.

A pond net is often placed a few hundred yards east of the south sand point of York Island.

Fisheries:

Lake Trout trolling is good during the summer around York Island shoals $2\frac{1}{2}$ miles north of York Island. The northwest edge of York Island shoals are marked by black can buoy #1. Trout fishing is also good in the summer near the Sand Island shoals of red nun buoy #2 (also known as the "Sevona pole").

The setting of a pond net.   *Photo by Claire Duquette*

Camping:

Because of eagle nesting and other variable situations, York Island's camping status should be checked with the Park Service.

The Vicinity:

A mile south of York Island is the mainland at Point Detour, the location for the Point Detour campground, a part of the Red Cliff Indian Reservation. Southeast of York Island, two miles across the west channel, lies Raspberry Island. During the day, one sees the white duplex of the Raspberry Lighthouse keeper's quarters overlooking the channel. From dusk to dawn, one sees the flashing white light of the Raspberry Island navigation light. Below the clay banks, one can see the white boathouse and dock. Beyond Raspberry and above it stands Oak Island, tallest of the Apostle Islands. Four miles northeast of York is Bear Island, the second tallest island. Beyond Bear lies Otter Island. North of Bear, about eight miles from York, is Devils Island, whose lighthouse flashes red at night. Devils Island is the northernmost point of land in Wisconsin. Several miles north of Devils Island are the shipping channels for east and west-bound traffic. Both ore carriers and salt water ships might be seen going to and from the Superior-Duluth twin ports. Forty-five miles north of York Island, on the north shore of Lake Superior, is the city of Taconite Harbor, Minnesota. Sand Island is two miles to the west. And to the southwest, on the mainland, one finds Little Sand Bay, the National Park Service Information Center, the Little Sand Bay dock and the Hokenson Fishery display.

Pride of Baltimore, a visiting schooner.
Photo by Claire Duquette.

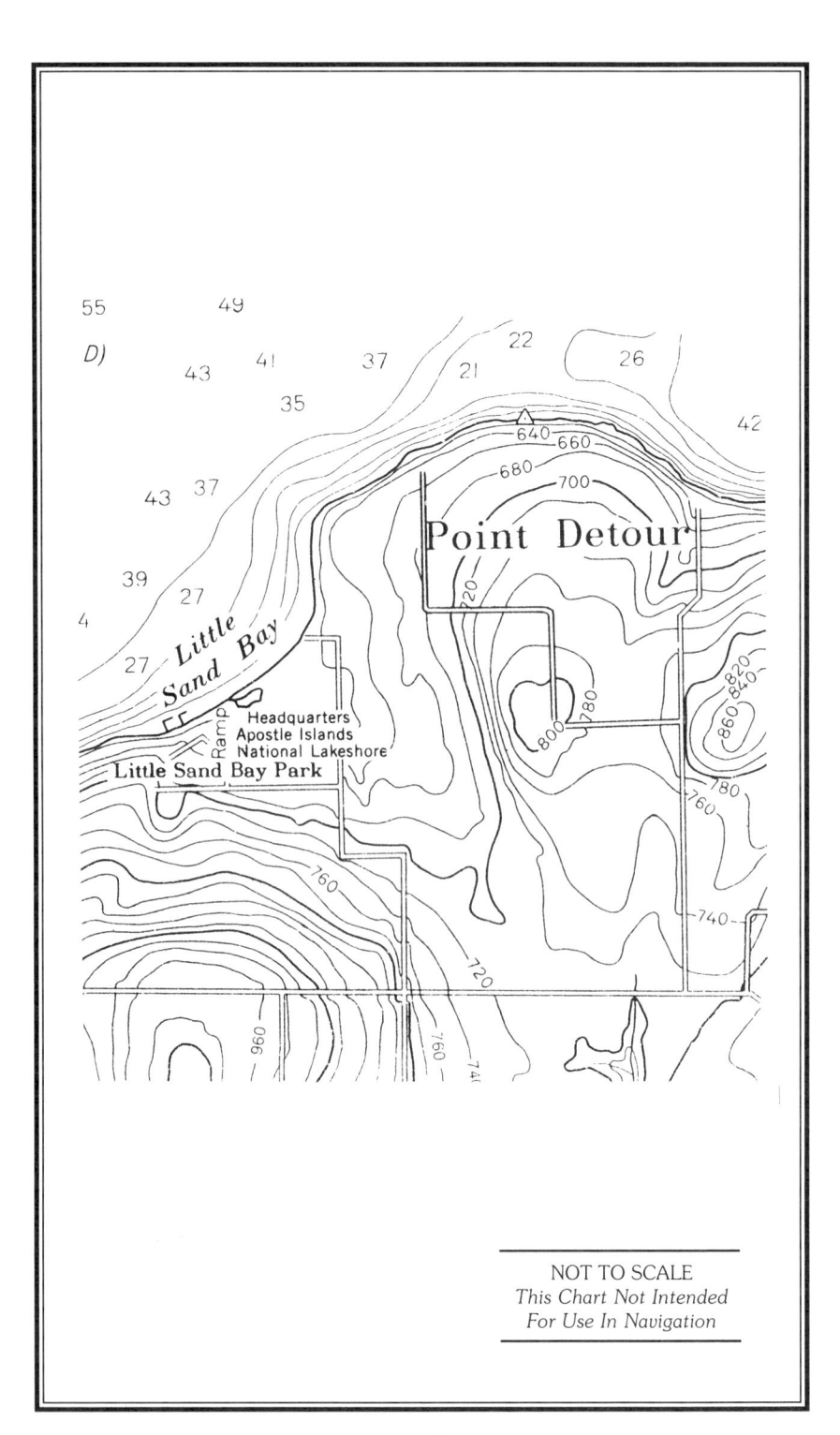

NOT TO SCALE
This Chart Not Intended For Use In Navigation

Little Sand Bay

Location:
   Little Sand Bay is located at the northernmost end of the Bayfield Peninsula. A long picturesque sand beach extends about a mile from east to west in this bay. Facing northward, one sees York and Sand Islands, open lake and the Minnesota shore 30 to 40 miles distant. Sand Bay, the mouth of the Sand River, lies 2 miles to the west, but Little Sand Bay is where most of the settlement activity took place over recent years.

Historic Sites:
   Two docks jut out into the lake from Little Sand Bay. The one to the east was part of Herman Johnson's fishery and resort and is now maintained by the Park Service. Above the Johnson dock, one will find the building which was formerly a small store serving the people of this locale as well as a number of resort visitors. At present, the building is a Visitor Information Center with several displays. National Park Service personnel are usually available at the Center throughout the season to assist visitors. Outside the Visitor Information Center, a large anchor from the sunken ore carrier SEVONA is on display. the anchor was lifted and brought to Little Sand Bay by Herman Johnson and friends and was donated to the National Park. A picture and the story of the tragedy of the SEVONA are shown on a plaque. The SEVONA was the ill-fated 3,166-ton ship which sank after breaking up on the Sand Island Shoals $4\frac{1}{2}$ miles north of Little Sand Bay in September, 1905.
   The dock to the west, called the Hokenson Fishing Dock, has been restored and stabilized as a historic place. The Hokenson fishing boat

The schooner Quickstep, one of the attractive classic boats of the Apostle Islands.
Photo by J. Peters

TWILITE is located here as part of a museum, showing a Lake Superior Fishery of the 1930's to '40's era, displaying authentic artifacts, tools, equipment, clothing and furnishings that were once part of the working fishery. Attached to the dock is a herring storage building containing exhibits of tools and equipment used in the harvesting, cleaning and packing of the herring. At the end of the dock is an ice house which was used to store ice cut from the lake in the winter. Above the beach is the net storage shed showing the processes used in making, mending, drying and storing nets, and in manufacturing wood floats. The museum depicts a fishery of the period from 1927 to 1962. Interpretive tours of the museum led by Park Naturalists are scheduled at various times throughout the day.

Moorage and Docking:

Short-term docking is allowed at the east dock on a space available basis. The depth of the water at the end of the dock is about 5 feet, but is variable. Currents in the Little Sand Bay area pile sand up inside the dock so boaters approaching the dock from either side should post a lookout to judge water depths. The sand bottom throughout the bay allows very good anchorage – and the locale offers some of the most magnificent sunsets anywhere on Lake Superior.

Camping:

Camping is permitted at the Town of Russell Park southeast of the Park Visitors Center. A tribal campground – Point Detour Campground is located about a mile east of Little Sand Bay at Point Detour.

Picnicking may be done along the beach and at the picnic sites between the docks.

Fisheries:

Trolling for brown trout is often done at the mouth of the Sand River and also around Sand Island.

Waterfalls off the islands are plentiful after rains.

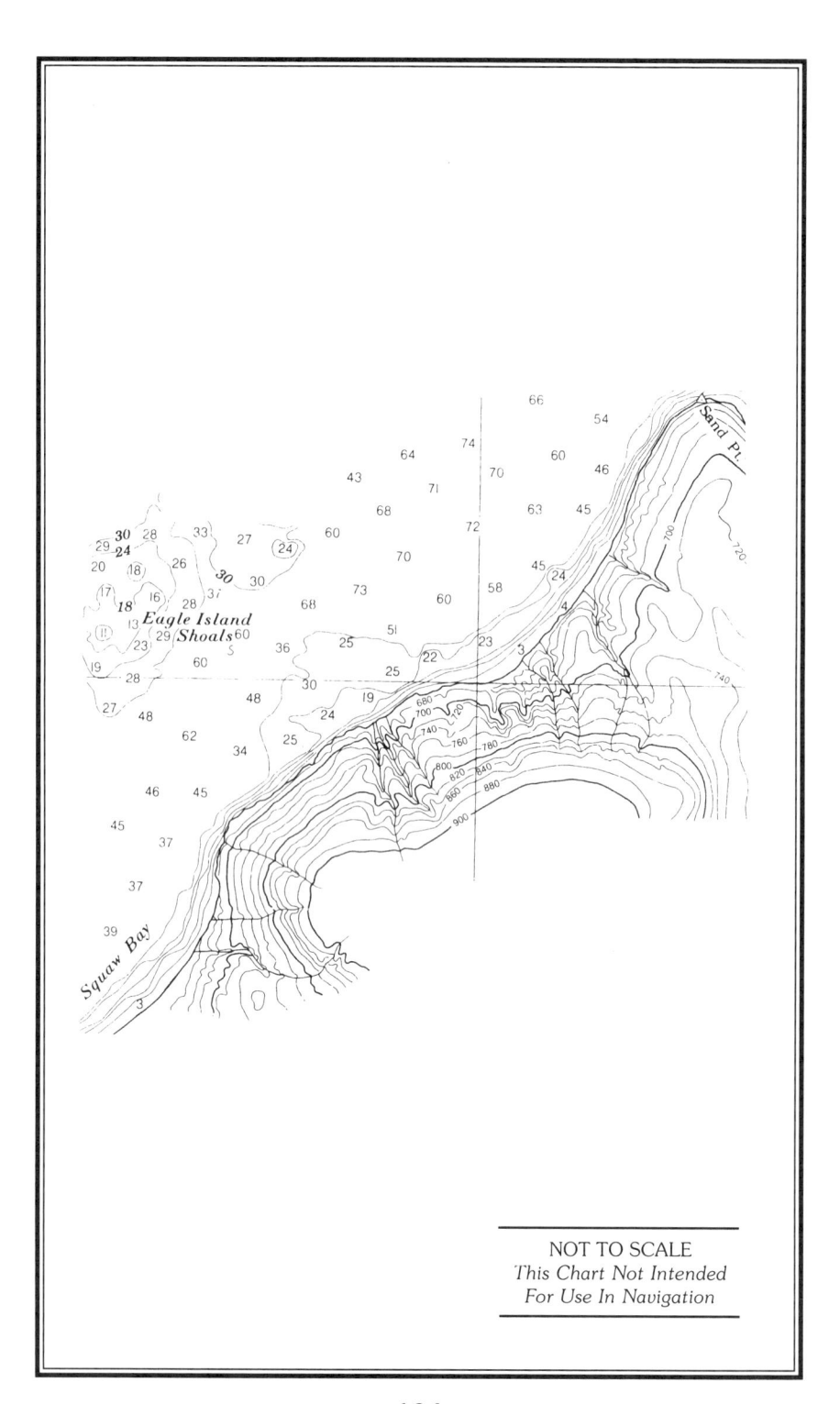

NOT TO SCALE
*This Chart Not Intended
For Use In Navigation*

Squaw Bay Caves

The Squaw Bay sea caves are located about three and a half miles southwest of Sand Island on the mainland. The caves extend along about two miles of the sandstone cliffs. Eroded caves are cut back into the cliffs from a few feet to 60 feet and more in some places. It is possible to enter some of these caves with small craft and to pass beneath arches of sandstone. A boater in the vicinity would miss one of the most beautiful features of the National Lakeshore if he passed up the opportunity to visit these caves. Obviously, the caves should be visited only when the seas and winds favor approaching the steep cliffs. Water depths drop off abruptly below the face of the cliffs, but a bow lookout is a good idea if one wishes to come in close.

During July and August, an excursion boat departs Bayfield for a tour of the shoreline on an evening cruise past the Sand Island Lighthouse and along the Sand Bay caves. It is scheduled to be cruising during the spectacular Sand Bay sunset.

The Vicinity:

The Village of Cornucopia lies about four miles west of Squaw Bay. One can find docking, lodging, food and beverages at "Corny," the northernmost village in Wisconsin.

Red Cliff buoy #4 along the west channel.

IV.
Boating Among the Islands

Schooner Zeeto is a bald-headed three-masted schooner built in 1954, imported to the Great Lakes in the 1990's.

The Lake Superior Scene – Waters, Wind, Weather

Lake Superior is an inland sea, the largest body of fresh water in the world. A few observations about Lake Superior should encourage one to appreciate the respect local boatmen give it.

Lake Superior has a surface of 31,800 square miles, a length of 350 miles, and a width of 160 miles. It is 1,332 feet deep at a location about 45 miles northeast of Marquette, Michigan.

Hydrologists have determined that one-eighth of all the fresh water in the world is found in Lake Superior. The average annual temperature of this water is less than 40 degrees, though waters in bays and shallows are often warmer. Thirty feet below the surface of the lake, water temperatures seldom vary more than 8 degrees year around.

Longfellow's Hiawatha called the lake "Gitchee Gumee," meaning "Shining Big Sea Water."

A combination of the lake's characteristics create the "lake effect," climatological differences which are sometimes drastic and abrupt. The cold water and the cool air above this water often react with the flow of warm inland air. These temperature differences result in a variety of contrasting weather conditions: fog, high winds, cool breezes and violent storms.

Some of the abnormalities in the generally temperate climate of northern Wisconsin include hot spring days with temperatures in the 90's a mile inland; in the 40's on the lake; snowfall on the Fourth of July; inland violent windstorms that can carry green leaves from trees on shore 2 miles distant; fog banks and patches; hail storms with golf ball and baseball-sized hailstones; and static electricity in the air raising your hair. It might, at this point, strike you that this is paradise for a distinctly masochistic strain of pleasure boaters. Not so. Those conditions are unusual and fortunately rare.

About 80% of all pleasure craft among the Apostle Islands are sailboats.

But they are real. What is also real is that 90 percent of our summer days will offer the outdoors person rare, superb beauty – rainbows floating above a dark blue lake, blazing red sunsets that linger forever, painting the sky and the water countless hues of the spectrum, Northern Lights that dance and flash across the night sky, and splashing sunny days with air so pure you inhale it for refreshment.

Now back to the hard core.

Lake Superior and the Boater

The most important single bit of information for boaters is the fact that the lake's weather sometimes changes radically and abruptly. Impending changes can often be seen in advance, sometimes not. Squall lines are made up of dark clouds and dark water. They normally come from the west or southwest. Watching the sky and water for these changes and sensing shifts in the breeze can help one develop a "weather eye." It is unusual for a person who spends most of his life indoors to develop a "weather eye," but a deliberate effort to develop a weather sense will serve a boater well on the lake. There are, of course, practical precautions and specific aids to anticipate the weather.

The Boat

One practical, precautionary consideration is the size of the boat. Most Great Lakes boaters feel small craft on the lake should be at least 18 to 20 feet in length with greater freeboard than needed on inland lakes. Deep-V and V-hulled boats are best suited for the choppy waters of the lake. Except within bays and near immediate refuge, canoes, cartop boats and small sailboats should not venture on the lake.

Engines on Lake Superior boats should be matched to the demands of strong winds and rough seas. Many Great Lakes boaters have twin engines or have an auxiliary engine for emergencies. Coast Guard publication "EMERGENCY REPAIRS AFLOAT (CG-179)" lists spare parts and tools that should be on board.

Also keep in mind that distances between islands are often deceiving and that fuel requirements might run a little higher when you are bucking wind and waves. There are no facilities among the islands for refueling.

While cruising on Lake Superior, the boater is regulated by U.S. Coast Guard as well as state laws. You must comply with the Great Lakes Rules of the Road and be able to understand navigation aids and channel markers. Certain equipment is required on all small craft, depending on their size and method of propulsion. One can request a courtesy examination from the Coast Guard or Coast Guard Auxiliary to be sure equipment is adequate.

Finally, the boater should make a "float plan" or "cruise plan" and file it with a responsible party on shore. It should include basic information and need not be formal or exhaustive. The CG publication "FEDERAL REQUIREMENTS FOR RECREATIONAL BOATERS (CG-290)" contains one of the best examples of a float plan.

The float plan can be left with a marina operator, a relative, friend or other responsible person. The plan will help the Coast Guard or other search and rescue units locate you if you are overdue. Keep a copy for yourself along with any notations about who you will or can call if there is a change in your plans. Get the proper radio names and/or call numbers of your contacts: e.g., Apostle Islands Marina.

Water taxis provide transportation to remote islands.

U.S. Coast Guard Float Plan Form

1. Name of person reporting _____ phone number _____
2. Description of boat: type _____ color _____
   Registration number _____
   Length _____ name _____ make _____
   Other information _____
3. Persons aboard _____
       name   age   address & phone number

4. Engine type _____ h.p. _____
   No. of engines _____ Fuel capacity _____
5. Survival equipment: Check as appropriate
   ❏ PFDs   ❏ flares   ❏ smoke signals   ❏ mirror   ❏ flashlight
   ❏ paddles   ❏ water   ❏ food   ❏ other
6. Radio ❏ yes ❏ no   type _____ frequencies_____
7. Trip expectations: Leave at _____ (time)
   From _____ going to _____
   Expect to return by _____ (time) and in no event later than_____
8. Other appropriate information _____
9. Automobile   License _____ type _____
   Trailer   license _____ color and make of auto _____
   Where parked _____
10. If not returned by _____ (time) call the Coast Guard, or _____

What to do about the Weather

    The National Oceanic and Atmospheric Administration informs us that prevailing winds come from the northeast during May, June and August. From September through April and in July, prevailing winds come from the west and northwest. July winds average 10-12 knots, with peak occurring about mid-afternoon. Early mornings and evenings are usually calm.

    Daily variations will obviously occur. To better prepare the boater, daily weather reports can be obtained from several sources, the best, most

Storms affecting the Apostle Islands Region

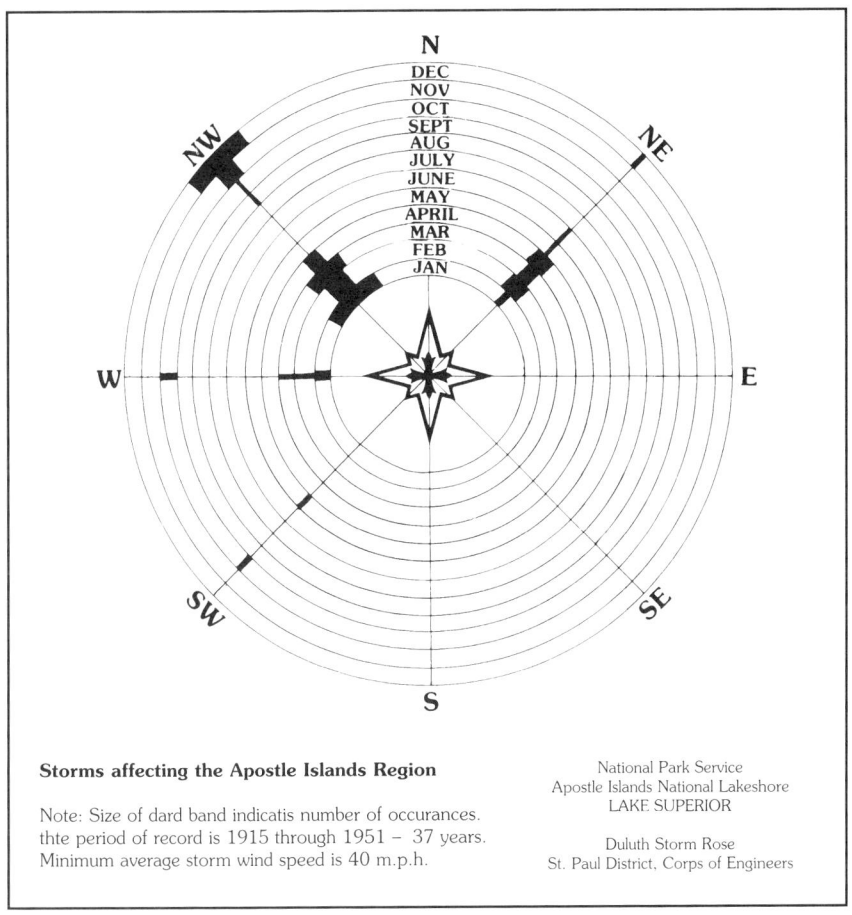

Note: Size of dard band indicatis number of occurances. thte period of record is 1915 through 1951 – 37 years.
Minimum average storm wind speed is 40 m.p.h.

National Park Service
Apostle Islands National Lakeshore
LAKE SUPERIOR

Duluth Storm Rose
St. Paul District, Corps of Engineers

current and appropriate being the Marine Weather for the Western Half of Lake Superior. Comparing the current Marine Weather broadcast for the Western Half of Lake Superior with what you actually see around you as you stand outdoors in the Western Half of Lake Superior can, to state it politely, show remarkable dissimilarities. Bear in mind that the West Half of Lake Superior is large, that the Apostle Islands lie somewhat within the bay and are relatively protected, that the lake effect is more noticeable near shore and that, as a result, weather conditions often vary greatly from place to place.

Now what does the boater in paradise do if the "best" is so questionable? Before cruising, check the marine forecast. Then, en route, check it periodically. Though weather forecasts can be received on AM or FM public radio, the best source of weather information comes via VHF-FM broadcasts. If the boat is equipped with the VHF-FM marine radio, one listens for announcements of marine weather up-dates every three hours by the Coast

Guard over Channel 16, with the broadcast following usually on Channel 22. Storm warnings are broadcast on WX-1 or WX-2 of the VHF-FM radio. If a boater has missed these means of obtaining weather information, call the local Coast Guard station and request a weather up-date. The National Park Headquarters in Bayfield often has access to current weather through their personnel stationed on the islands.

Fog can occur in patches or in vast regions of the lake. If one does not need to travel through it, it is best to wait it out. If trapped in fog, rely on compass and navigation chart. Small craft should have radar reflectors so that they can be detected by boats with radar. Also, sound appropriate fog signals while under way at a moderate speed.

Doubtless, there are more than a mere handful of boaters whose hearts have ping-ponged around inside their chest cavities when the ghost of a boat suddenly materialized in front of them in a fog.

If a storm approaches, the boater should head for shelter, a harbor, a dock, or get behind an island, anchoring when it appears reasonable, simply maintaining a heading when anchoring is not feasible. Though it only happens occasionally, storm winds can change directions 180° so getting behind an island doesn't usually call for cocktails and card games below decks until the storm passes. If one cannot make it to protected water, the boat should be headed into the wind and waves at about a 45-degree angle at enough speed to maintain steerage and control. Life jackets should be put on. Passengers and load should be centered and kept low. Water should be kept out by closing hatches or pumping.

If engine failure occurs (and storms are when filters get clogged and water in the fuel enters the carburetor, creating engine failure), a sea anchor (bucket, or a bulky object that will scoop water) trailed on a line from the bow will keep the bow into the waves. This is when you pull out your tool kit and spare parts. And, being thoroughly familiar with your engine, you fault trace. Attempt to make repairs but also have someone keep track of what your boat is doing. If you are certain you need assistance you can call another boat for immediate aid or call the Coast Guard to be rescued. If you have no radio, use your flares, but only when you know you will be seen. If you have no flares, raising and lowering arms or a bright object, such as a jacket, at a passing boat is a sign of distress. Rapid blasts on your horn or whistle is another distress call. If all this is happening and you're just now reading your alternatives, you'd best put away this book, empty one of the bottles on board, jot a nautical farewell along with an apology to the EPA, curl the note up, tuck it in the bottle, cap it up, and toss it overboard.

What you were supposed to do before this storm was this:

Plan a program of preventative maintenance on your boat. Have on board tools and spare parts the Coast Guard listed. Plan for Emergencies: engine failure, fire, sinking, violent storms, medical emergency, man overboard. If you are going to enjoy your boat, practice – or at least think through – your handling of these emergencies one at a time, and then in combination.

Finally, one of the most important things to consider is the temperature of the water – whether you fall into it, jump into it, it splashes you, or simply cools the air that cools you. Because of the low water temperature and the cooling effect of the wind, hypothermia or exposure is an ever-present danger on Lake Superior.

The Great Lakes Sea Grant Network publication A BOATER'S GUIDE TO LAKE SUPERIOR LAUNCH RAMPS has this to say about hypothermia:

Hypothermia is another name for exposure, an ever-present danger on Lake Superior. It is a lowering of the body's core temperature (98.6°F) caused by the immersion in cold water (less than 70°F) or, out of the water, by a combination of wet, cold, and windy weather. If the body's core temperature drops more than 20°F, death will soon follow.

Even during the hottest summer weather, water temperature seldom reaches 55°F, except in shallow bays and sunny beaches. If a person falls into the lake at 55°F, survival time without a personal floatation device (PFD) would average less than two hours.

To increase survival time:

A PFD will increase your chances of survival for two reasons: it will keep you afloat and will retain body heat.

Try to climb back in or on top of your craft. The more of your body you can get out of the water, the better off you will be, since water takes heat away from the body 25 times faster than air at the same temperature. In addition, you will be easier to spot by anyone searching for you.

If you can't climb back into the craft, but are wearing the PFD, curl your body up by tucking in your knees and keeping your arms as close to your sides as possible. This will decrease heat loss from the three most vulnerable areas – the head, ribcage, and groin – and double your survival time.

Do not try to swim to shore unless you are within a mile of it and no other help is available. *The average swimmer wearing a PFD is capable of swimming no more than a mile in 50° water before succumbing to hypothermia.*

If you rescue someone who has been in the water for any length of time:

Get the victim out of the wind and rain. If the victim is in the water, try to avoid being pulled in yourself.

Replace wet clothing with dry clothes.

If the victim is conscious, give hot, sweet drinks. *Under no circumstances should alcohol be used, since it speeds up the heat loss of the body.*

If the person is semi-conscious or worse, try to keep him or her awake. If there is difficulty in breathing, ensure an open air passage. Administer mouth-to-mouth resuscitation if breathing stops altogether.

Rewarm the victim by the best possible method; use body-to-body contact in a sleeping bag, a heated room, or if possible, use a hot bath (105-110°F), leaving the limbs out.

Seek immediate medical attention.

A Few Observations about Anchoring

Anchorages among the islands span the possibilities from occasional to relatively secure. Wind, waves, the skill of the skipper, bottom characteristics and the quality of equipment all bear on the security of an anchorage.

Anchoring overnight off a secluded beach or in a remote cove can be one of the truly peak experiences of a boater among the islands. As in many adventures, the effort and the risk are what make it unique, uncommon and uncrowded. The risk can be minimized by learning a few fundamentals of anchoring and by PRACTICING THEM ahead of time.

1. Know the characteristics and holding power of your anchors and tackle.
2. Plan your anchor rode and mark its length with a tape or ribbon. Scopes 5:1 are minimal, 7:1 are good.
3. Plan your anchorage in advance, keeping water conditions and water depths in mind.
4. Know several ways to anchor.
5. Notice how other boats are anchored, planning your own scope and swinging radius accordingly.
6. Set your anchor carefully, consider placing two, and plan how to raise them.
7. Check your position after anchoring and watch other boats which might anchor after you.
8. Plan what you are going to do at 3:00 a.m. when the winds switch 180 degrees, rain slicks the deck, winds gust to 50 mph, and you want to continue enjoying your cruise.
9. Don't let what MIGHT happen – rain, storms, pestilence, plague – ruin your good times among the Apostle Islands. Make thoughtful planning part of your challenge – and enjoy!

The three-masted schooner Zeeto cruises daily May through the end of September. A great variety of vessels pass through the islands from voyageur canoes to chinese junks.

*Public Docks in the Apostle Islands National Lakeshore

Map Symbol	Location	Name	Water Depth (Outer End)	Description
①	Stockton Island	Presque Isle Point Dock	7'	concrete, L-shaped
②	Stockton Island	Quarry Bay Dock	4'	wood, shallow
③	Basswood Island	West Side Dock	4-5'	wood
④	Rocky Island	Park Service Dock	over 6'	wood
⑤	Outer Island	Lighthouse Dock	5'	concrete, rocky bottom
⑥	Devils Island	Northeast Landing	6'	natural rock ledge (CAUTION)
⑦	Devils Island	South Landing	5'	wood, small harbor
⑧	Raspberry Island	Lighthouse Dock	5-6'	wood, rocky bottom
⑨	Sand Island	East Bay Dock	4-5'	wood, sandy bottom
⑩	South Twin Island	Norht Dock	4-5'	wood
⑪	South Twin Island	South Dock	6-7'	wood
⑫	Oak Island	West Side Dock	6-7'	wood
⑬	Little Sand Bay	Park Service Dock	5-6'	wood, L-shape

NOTE: No totally protected docks or mooring areas exist among the islands. Boaters should keep advised as to storm warnings or wind direction changes. Water depth may change drastically due to sudden storms.

* Other docks within the National Lakeshore are private. Please do not trespass.

Suggested Safe Anchorage Areas Within The Apostle Islands National Lakeshore

Map Symbol	Location	Name
⑭	Stockton Island	Anderson Bay
⑮	Raspberry Island	East Bay
⑯	Rocky Island	Park Service Dock Area

Area Marinas & Boat Launch Facilities

Map Symbol	Name
⑰	Apostle Islands Marina
⑱	Department of Natural Resources Boat Launch
⑲	Port Superior Marina
⑳	Madeline Island Yacht Club
㉑	Red Cliff Marina
㉒	Schooner Bay Marina
㉓	Town of Russell Boat Launch

A Summary of Docks and Anchorages of the Apostle Islands National Lakeshore

Basswood Island: West side dock, 71' wood crib, approximately 50' useable both sides, 4-5' water depth offshore end, sand bottom.

Stockton Island: Presque Isle dock, 250' concrete, approximately 160' useable inside only, 7' deep outer end, time limits posted, NPS reserved portion, Ranger residents, excellent anchorages to north. Precaution: irregular sand bottom, shallows, submerged crib 150' NE of end of dock. Quarry Bay dock, 95' wood crib, 70' useable both sides, 4' deep end, hazardous in south wind, sand bottom, excellent anchorages in bay. Julian Bay, excellent anchorage in appropriate wind conditions, sand bottom, very scenic. Precautions: wind shift, irregular bottom.

Oak Island: West side dock, 120' wood crib, 80' useable both sides. 6-7' deep end, south side shallower, sand bottom. Precautions: sand bar about 100' offshore of dock changes yearly in depth and location.

Raspberry Island: West side Lighthouse dock, 30' inside, rocky bottom, 60' outside, 5-6' deep outside end. Precautions: westerly winds, rocky bottom, rocks along shore south of dock. Anchorage, East Bay sand point, sand bottom. Precautions: pond net south of west dock, wind shifts.

Sand Island: East Bay, 200' wood crib, 100' useable each side, 4-5' deep end of dock, sand bottom, anchorage in vicinity. Justice Bay – anchorage in appropriate wind, sand and rock bottom. West Bay – anchorage in appropriate wind, sand bottom. Precautions: rocks off drainage area, east side of bay; rocks north side of bay. Lighthouse Bay – anchorage during appropriate wind conditions, sand bottom.

Little Sand Bay: L-shaped wood crib, 120' inside of L, 165' both sides of landward leg, 5-6' irregular sand bottom, reserved portion, useable portion good under proper wind conditions, anchorage in vicinity. Precautions, shallow water inside L.

Rocky Island: 220' wooden crib, 140' and 170' useable two sides, reserved portion and time limits, sand bottom, over 6' deep. Ranger residence. Anchorage in vicinity of NPS dock, sand bottom.

South Twin Island: North Dock, 30' useable, 45' deep. South Dock 30' useable two sides, 6-7' deep, sand and cobble bottom.

Devils Island: South Landing, small harbor inside 175', approximately 100' useable, rocky bottom, 5' deep end. Precautions: weather. Northeast landing, rock ledge, approximately 50' useable, 6' deep. Precaution: rock outcroppings, wind. This is a tentative landing.

Outer Island: North end, concrete dock and breakwater, 100' dock useable, 5' deep. Precaution: rocky bottom, irregular waves from open lake. This is a tentative docking.

Michigan Island: L-shaped, very changeable conditions and shifting bottom sands.

Marine Facilities in the Apostle Islands Area

Apostle Islands Marina, Bayfield
VHF Radio – Channel 16
   Overnight docking, long term docking. 30 ton hoist, gas and diesel fuel, mechanic, supplies, showers.
   Vicinity – City of Bayfield, groceries, on/off liquor, dining, laundry, motels, sailboat charters, transportation to islands, municipal boat ramp, outfitters, information, fishing supplies, National Lakeshore Headquarters.

Madeline Island Yacht Club, LaPointe, Madeline Island
VHF Radio – Channel 16
   Overnight docking, ramp gas to diesel fuel, repair facility, hoist, showers, supplies.
   Vicinity – on/off liquor, dining, groceries, golf, motel, sail repair.

Port Superior Marina, 3 miles south of Bayfield
VHF Radio – Channel 16
   Overnight docking, 30 ton hoist, ramp, gas and diesel fuel, repair facility, supplies.
   Vicinity – dining, on/off liquor, swimming pool, condominiums, sailboat charters. Approach channel: north end of breakwater, between channel markers.

Roys Point Marina, 2 miles north of Bayfield, docking, fuel.

Red Cliff Marina, Red Cliff, 2.5 miles north of Bayfield
   Overnight docking, ramp, gas.
   Vicinity – camping, casino

Schooner Bay Marina, Red Cliff Bay, $3\frac{1}{2}$ miles north of Bayfield
   Overnight docking, long term docking, gas, mechanic, showers.

Cornucopia
   Harbor, overnight docking, gas.
   Vicinity – dining, liquor.

Washburn
   Boat ramp.
   Vicinity – City center, laundry, dining, liquor, motel, groceries.
   Washburn Marina: 150-ton hoist, gas and diesel fuel, overnight and long-term docking, large vessel repair facility, supplies, showers.

Madeline Island Yacht Club and Marina, the Village of LaPointe dock and ferry landing.

Schooner Bay Marina, three miles north of Bayfield.

Port Superior Marina, two miles south of Bayfield.

Red Cliff Marina, fuel dock, and Red Cliff Arts & Crafts Center.

Roy's Point Marina, Bayfield.

Apostle Islands Marina, City Dock, City of Bayfield.

About Beaching a Boat on an Island or How Not to Make the Same Mistakes I Made

Beaching is one of the more expedient means of gaining access to some of the beautifully secluded sand beaches within the Lakeshore. No other place gives quite the same kind of aloneness as being on a small private beach looking out over a mile or two of calm Lake Superior. Landing at these spots requires certain risks – risk of bumping bottom with propeller, risk of being grounded when a swell lifts you farther than you wanted to go up on the beach, and there are times when safe beaching is not even possible.

I have picked camping parties off beaches in 4 and 5 foot waves, getting away unscratched and unscathed with nothing but a good story to tell. I have also gone into a dead calm beach and backed away with twisted outdrives and nicked propellers. You, too, can enjoy nicked propellers and twisted outdrives. But in case you'd rather not, here are some suggestions:

Select a beach cautiously. Post a bow lookout as you ease your boat toward the beach. Generally, rocks will be found in the water if they are found along the beach. But not always. Sometimes they are just waiting for you to find them. A bow lookout should have a notion of how objects and their depths are distorted by clear water. It will be useful for the lookout to have a weighted line or a pike pole to establish depths and also to fend off from rocks that sneak up. It's good to establish some basic voice and hand signals, e.g., "Rock dead ahead," "Dead head to port," "Mark Twain," etc. Once you establish that you can land without damaging your outdrives, shafts, propellers, etc., back off, drop a kedge and set it, then ease yourself back in to the beach while paying out the line. When you are where you want to be, secure the line on a cleat. Tie another line on the bow, preparing to secure it to an object ashore. Go back to the stern line. If you can put some tension on the stern line and then go forward and tie your bow line, the boat will be pulled free of the sand as the tension takes up line and the boat will float rather than grind in the sand.

Keep in mind that wind/wave conditions change and the skipper's head should lie restless in direct proportion to the mortgage/cost/insurance/pucker factor. When it is time to depart, put belongings and garbage on board, climb aboard with the bow line, and pull yourself out with the stern line on the kedge, lift the kedge, and resume your cruise. Bon voyage.

Sometimes a brief stay does not call for the kedge or the accompanying rituals. But bear in mind, many skippers have gone swimming after boats that defy their hopes that keels resting on a sand beach are secure. A line to shore is a good idea.

Once again, the conditions to keep in mind are the rocks, the wake of passing vessels, wind shifts, and how to get off the beach gracefully. The uniqueness of island beaches will leave a lasting memory – a good one if you observe a few precautions on beaching.

A shoreline among the Apostle Islands – rugged sandstone laid down 600 million years ago.

V.

Marine Radio Communications

The increasing amount of boat traffic in the Apostle Islands region has affected marine radio communications – in some ways to the better, in some ways worse. Perhaps a brief account of a recent incident will demonstrate one or two problems and the seriousness of the consequences of misuse of the radio.

On a particularly busy weekend radio traffic was frequently being interrupted by a child using a marine radio as a toy. He was answering calls that were not directed to him, he was keying the microphone and broadcasting music, and was generally interrupting regular traffic. These interruptions continued on the the greater part of the day. Somewhere about mid-afternoon, an ore ship sent a distress call. From portions which the child did not disrupt, local boaters could piece together parts of the distress call: a seaman had jumped overboard from the vessel and the ore carrier was obviously seeking assistance and would not be able to stop and rescue the man overboard for at least the time it took the vessel to come about. Specific information being transmitted by the ore boat was superseded by the child shouting, "Help! Help me! S.O.S.," and various other interfering transmissions.

Such incidents generate enough resentful anger to power a radio transmission on their own energy.

Radios are licensed by the Federal Communications Commission to responsible adults and, when used by a child, must be used in the presence of the adult licensee.

The Coast Guard publication, MARINE COMMUNICATIONS FOR THE RECREATIONAL BOATER, outlines the types of marine communications systems, tells how to use marine radiotelephone, and gives distress communication procedures.

Types of Marine Communication Systems

The boating public has three communication systems, or bands, from which to choose: the 2-3 Megahertz (MHz) Radiotelephone band, the Very High Frequency-Frequency Modulated (VHF-FM) Maritime Mobile band, and the Citizens Band (CB). NOTE – CB is NOT strictly a marine communications band and may be operated from ships, boats, cars, trucks, and fixed land stations.

In making your decision you should know that the 2-3 MHz and the VHF-FM bands have been officially designated and internationally recognized as "marine" communication bands. For this reason, the Coast Guard, and maritime rescue organizations throughout the world, continuously monitor the distress frequencies of these bands.

The Coast Guard also monitors the emergency channel for Citizens Band radio, but it is on a "not-to-interfere" basis with its primary responsibility for monitoring distress frequencies on the recognized marine bands. In other words, if the Coast Guard receives a distress call over the 2-3 MHz or VHF-FM bands, it may cease monitoring CB in order to devote its entire efforts to respond to the emergency. However, if the Coast Guard receives a distress call over the CB emergency channel, it will respond immediately, but it will not cease monitoring the distress frequencies of the designated marine communications bands.

The National Park Service also monitors Channel 16 and can be of assistance to boaters.

Marine weather forecasts are available from the National Weather Service on VHF-FM. Also, in some areas the Coast Guard will broadcast weather information on both 2-3 MHz and VHF-FM. You should contact the National Weather Service, your marina, or your boating equipment store for information on which channel serves the area you will be boating in.

How to Use Your Marine Radiotelephone

With the number of radio-equipped boats continuing to increase, it is important that each boater observe a few basic procedures when using the radio. These procedures are:

1. Prior to sailing, make sure your equipment is operating properly. Obtain a radio check. To do this you must call a specific station on a working frequency and, after establishing contact, ask "How do you hear me?" Radio checks on 2182 KHz are prohibited by law, and on VHF-FM channel 16 are strongly discouraged. The Coast Guard will not respond to a radio check on CB channel 9.

2. Be courteous. Always listen to see if the channel is clear before transmitting. Try not to cut into someone else's conversation.

3. When transmitting, always identify your boat by name and call sign.

4. Distress frequencies can be used to establish contact with another station, but after establishing contact you must shift to a working frequency unless you are in distress or have knowledge of a distress.

5. Complete all conversations as soon as practical. Don't tie up a frequency with "chit-chat."

6. Federal Communications Commission regulations require that boats equipped with 2-3 MHz and VHF-FM radiotelephone maintain a lis-

tening watch on 2182 KHz or channel 16, respectively, if the radio is turned on.

Distress Communications Procedures
1. Speak slowly and clearly.
2. Make sure your radio is turned on.
3. Turn to the distress frequency; channel 16 for VHF-FM, 2182 KHz for 2 MHz Radiotelephone, or channel 9 for Citizens Band.
4. Press microphone button and transmit: "Mayday, Mayday, Mayday."
5. Identify yourself by saying "This is (your boat's name), (your boat's name), (your boat's name), (your call sign)."
6. Give your position. Give as must information on your location as possible – landmarks which are near, longitude and latitude, etc.
7. Tell what is wrong.
8. Tell what kind of assistance you need.
9. Give the number of people who are aboard your boat and, if any are injured, their condition.
10. Give the estimated seaworthiness of your boat.
11. Give a description of your boat – length, type, color, number of masts, etc.
12. Tell which channel or frequency you will be listening on.
13. End your message with: "This is (your boat's name and call sign). Over."
14. Wait for a response. If no answer, repeat your call. If still no answer, try another channel or frequency.

NOTE: If the Coast Guard, or another rescue organization, responds to your call, you may be asked many questions that seem unnecessary. Every question is important, since each item of information increases your chances of rescue. If you are in immediate danger, help will be dispatched while the information is being taken.

The following is a listing of VHF-FM channels and their recommended purposes.
16 – Distress/safety/calling
06 – Intership/Safety use only
09 – Ship to Coast only (Ship to Marinas and Yacht Clubs)
10 – Intership/Ship to Coast (Commercial only)
12 – Ship to Coast Guard
14 – Ship to Coast Guard
22 – Ship to Ship and to Coast

26 – Ship to Public Coast
68 – Intership/Ship to Coast
WXI – Continuous Weather

It should be noted by the boater that all channels (and there are many more) have *stated* purposes, and that one does not simply use any channel for any purpose.

Citizens' Band (CB) broadcasting went "public" because the public wished to play with it. Marine telephones serve serious purposes – if only occasionally – and, along with the marine radio license, an intelligent intent of the user is assumed.

The Wisconsin Fish Hatchery supplies Lake Trout to the Apostle Islands as well as other lakes.

VI.

Fishing

The best source of information on net types, fish species harvested, and commercial fishing in general is found in the Department of Natural Resource's publication FISHING IN THE GREAT LAKES.

A stop at fish markets in Bayfield and Red Cliff can get you fresh and smoked fish. With these as a final resort, there is no excuse for getting skunked while fishing the Apostle Islands.

When to Fish the Lakes

Coho Salmon

Spring fishing is best near shore. By mid-June, wind direction and water temperatures dictate where the fish are. Migrating fish provide fishing near tributary streams beginning in early fall.

Brown Trout

Spring through fall shoreline fishing. Fall runs of migratory fish in tributary streams of Lake Superior. Lake Superior trolling is good in autumn off stream mouths. Ice fishing in bays round out the season.

Commercial fishing has been a mainstay of Apostle Islands settlers since almost every island had a summer fish camp in the 1930's and 1940's.

Photo by J. Strzok

Rainbow Trout

Spring runs of migrating rainbows begin in early March, spreading north as the season progresses. April is a good month on Lake Superior tributaries. Best fishing for fall-run rainbows is October and November. Trolling is good throughout summer.

Brook Trout

Limited spring fishing near shore and in tributary streams. Good catches in spring, early summer, and fall in near shore areas of Lake Superior.

Lake Trout

Trolling produces fish from May to mid-September, with fish moving further offshore or to deeper water as the season progresses and water temperatures increase. Ice fishing near Apostle Islands of Lake Superior from Christmas on. Splake, a hybrid lake trout, offers year-round fishing near shore in Lake Superior.

Walleye

May through October and winter months in and along the shore of Green Bay. Spring fishing in the St. Louis estuary (Lake Superior). Good fishing off port of Superior July to September.

Yellow Perch

April through October for all of Green Bay, with ice fishing January to March. Good summer pier and breakwater fishing in southern Lake Michigan. On Lake Superior, the Ashland area is good all year.

Smallmouth Bass

Mid-May through September near shore or reefs on the bay-side of Door County and west shore of Green Bay.

Smelt

Beginning in early April in southern Lake Michigan, extending northward as the month progresses. Lake Superior fishing begins in late April and runs through May.

Gill Net

The gill net acts as an invisible underwater barrier. Fish of a certain size become entangled, or "gilled," while smaller fish swim through and larger fish turn away.

The design is simple. Monofilament twine, woven into a network of diamond-shaped openings, is strung between two heavy cords. Lead weights hold down the bottom and floats keep the top up. An anchor holds the net in place, and a buoy marks its location on the water's surface.

Each net is 300-400 feet long, but they're fished in gangs as long as

15,000 feet. Hydraulic net litters haul them into the boat, where fish are untangled from the net and stored on board.

The gill net is very versatile, can be set on any bottom, at any depth, and will catch almost any fish. A disadvantage is that it is selective by size, not species of fish. This means that nontarget fish also get caught and are killed if badly entangled.

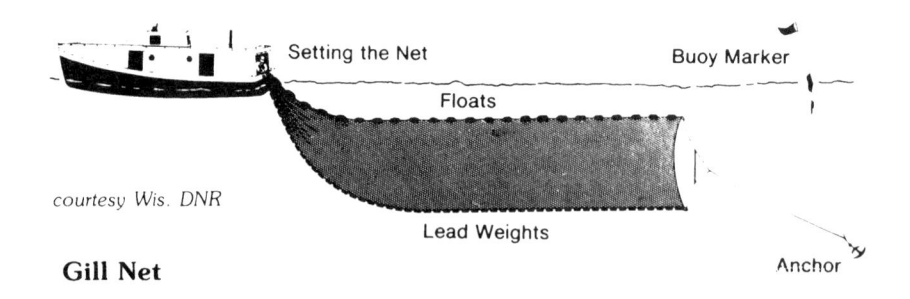

courtesy Wis. DNR

Gill Net

Setting the Net • Floats • Lead Weights • Buoy Marker • Anchor

Pound Net (also Pond Net)

The pound net is fished in water up to 90 feet deep. It works on the principle that fish will try to swim around a visible obstacle. The lead net, made of large-mesh twine, provides the obstacle. Fish swim along side it until they enter the heart through a small opening. Inside, they must either find their way back through the narrow opening or pass through the tunnel into the pot. Once in the pot, there is little chance for escape.

A special boat is used to remove trapped fish. With one side of the net temporarily lowered, the boat is pulled inside the pot. The sides and bottom of the net are gathered into the boat, bunching the fish toward the outside of the net. When they are concentrated in a small area, the catch is scooped on board.

Pound nets are large and heavy and are held in place by long stakes and anchors. Setting one is a big job, undertaken as seldom as possible. Picking the right location is very important. A successful net can produce thousands of pounds of fish in one day's lift.

Trap Net

The trap net is a comparatively small net, easily set and moved from one location to another. Fish swimming along the lead are funneled into the closed part of the net, first to the forebay and finally the pot. The wing-shaped hearts keep fish from straying as they move along the lead.

Once inside the pot, they remain trapped until the commercial fisher comes to scoop them out. To get at them, the net is heaved up onto the flat deck of a boat until the pot is accessible. A string sealing the pot is

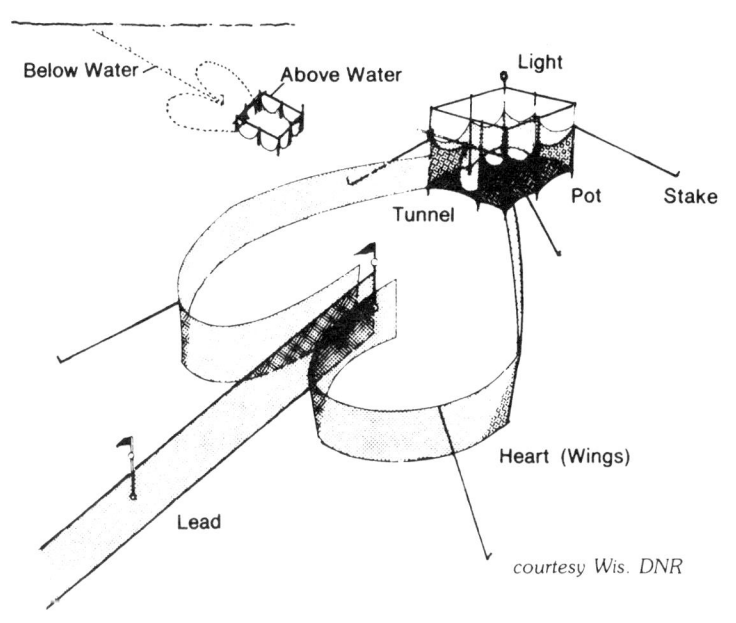

[Diagram labels: Below Water, Above Water, Light, Pot, Stake, Tunnel, Heart (Wings), Lead]

courtesy Wis. DNR

undone, and the fish are removed.

The fyke net (drop net), similar to the trap net but more rounded, is also used in Lake Michigan.

Trawl

Trawls are the most effective gear for the very abundant species such as alewives and smelt. They're relatively new to the Great Lakes, introduced in the early sixties.

The trawl's open end is weighted on the bottom and has floats on top to keep it open. Two boards, called otter doors, are attached to the open end. Riding along the bottom, these doors keep the net spread from left to right.

Recording depth sounders locate fish and help determine when to haul in the net. Power winches haul the catch on board, the end of the bag is untied, and the catch is dumped on deck for processing. The net is released off the back of the boat and another drag begins.

How to Fish the Lakes

Shore Fishing

Includes fishing from piers and breakwaters, wading, and still fishing from boats near shore. Best all-around tackle is a light to medium weight spinning rod. Spoons, plugs and spinner flies are popular artificial lures. Good natural baits are alewives, spawn sacks, and minnows. Fly fishing

Trap Net

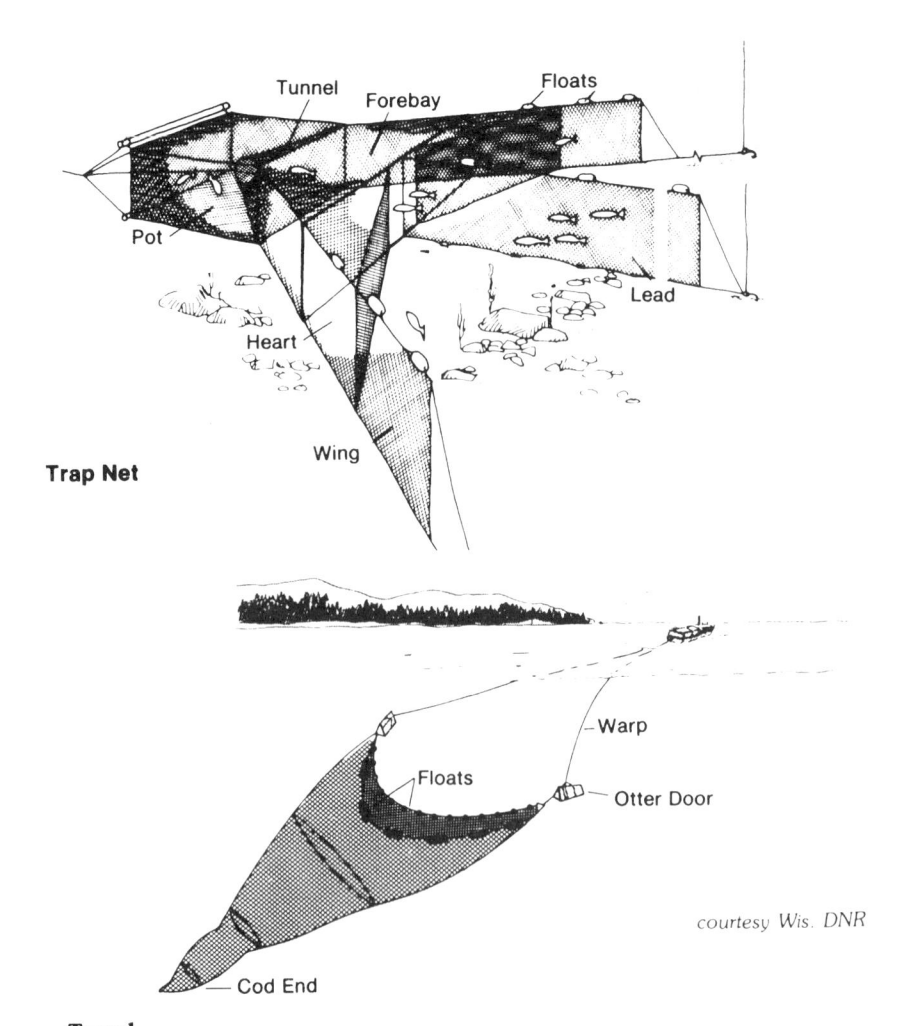

Trawl

courtesy Wis. DNR

with streamers can provide good action in bays and along rocky shorelines.

Special regulations allow salmon to be harvested by snagging each fall. Heavy duty fishing tackle, large reel, weighted treble hook and long-handled net are standard gear. Smelt provide another special fishery. Seines and nets are used to harvest them each spring on beaches and in and around tributary streams.

Stream Fishing

Spawning migrations of trout, salmon and walleye produce good fishing in tributary streams each spring and fall. Medium weight spinning tackle is most often used although fly fishing has an ample following. Spawn is

Fish tugs lay in the ice awaiting a March thaw at Apostle Islands Marina winter boat storage.

the most productive bait for trout and salmon. It can be fished as a single egg, egg cluster, or sack. Other natural baits and artificial lures are also used. Minnows or their imitations remain the best bait for walleye.

Trolling

Trolling is the most popular way to fish the open lake. A moving boat pulls up to six lines through the water, each attached to a rod mounted on the back of the boat. For deep trolling, special gear is needed to get the lure down. Downriggers, trolling

A Wisconsin Department of Natural Resources hatchery worker assembles a frame of astroturf layers, between which fertilized Lake Trout eggs are spread to be placed on traditional Lake Trout spawning reefs to assist replenishing the fish population.

131

planes, heavy sinkers, and wire lines each can do the job. A "flat line" is usually fished off the back of the boat for shallow trolling. Outriggers and ski boards are added to keep lines spread apart and away from engine noise.

Plugs, spoons, and flies are used for lures, often with a fish attractor attached. Fishing the right depth is a key to trolling success. Fish locators are standard gear on many boats, but finding the right water temperature can be just as effective. Trolling speed and pattern are also part of trolling "science."

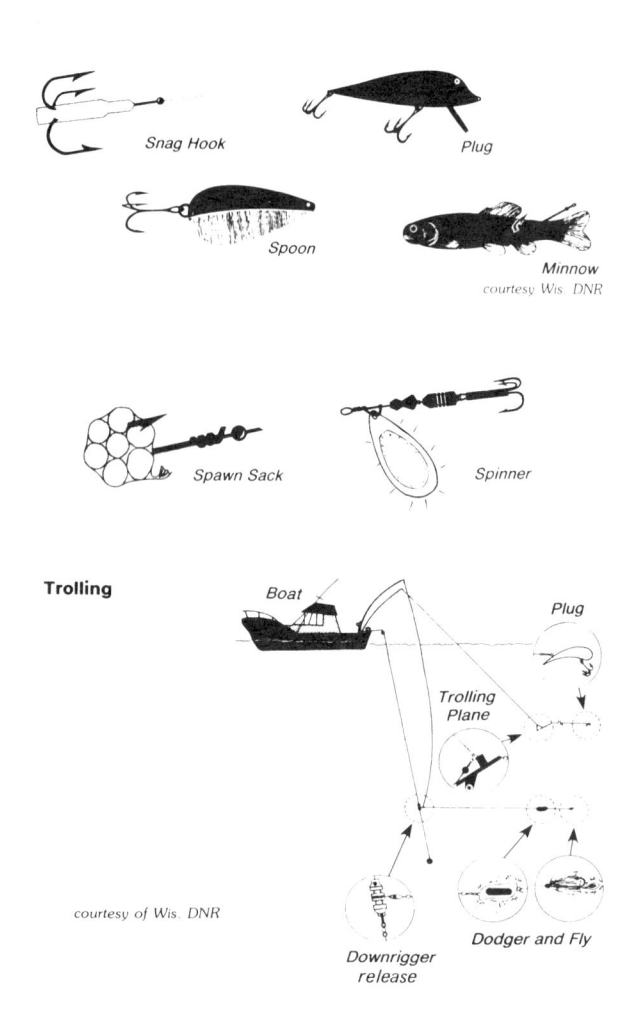

Fish tugs ply the Apostle Islands' waters from March through December fishing for Trout, Whitefish and Chubs.

VII.

Camping in the Apostle Islands National Lakeshore

Primitive camping areas have been designated on many islands within the Apostle Islands National Lakeshore. To help monitor camper use and impact, permits are required at all sites and are available from the Park offices at Little Sand Bay and Bayfield, and the island Ranger Stations.

Camping is only permitted in the designated areas. Some campsites have been designated with tent pads, tables, and grills. Where these facilities are furnished, camping is restricted to these sites. Where no facilities are provided, camping is permitted anywhere within the designated area.

Campfires must be build in fire pits or grills when provided. The gathering of wood for fuel is limited to downed wood. Fires should be attended and completely extinguished when no longer needed. The use of compact backpacking stoves is recommended. They are more efficient than wood fires and do not result in depletion of wood supplies.

No facilities for garbage are provided. It is recommended that only food in burnable packaging be used. Dehydrated and freeze dried foods packed in plastic or other burnable wrappings are lightweight, available in a good variety, and generally easy to prepare. All unburnable garbage must be packed out.

Some island campsites have wells but drinking water can be dipped from Lake Superior. Boiling the water for at least five minutes will assure its safe use. Common sense and regulations require that pollutants such as soapy water, fish entrails, human wastes, etc., not be deposited in the water. Burying of decomposable wastes at a safe distance from the water is recommended.

It is recommended that pets be left home. Regulations require all pets be under physical restrictive control.

Getting to the Islands

For those without boats, transportation is available from Bayfield. The Park Concessioner provides water taxi service to all islands. The Apostle Islands Cruise Service, Bayfield, Wisconsin has shuttle service to Stockton Island and other islands in addition to scheduled excursion trips.

The 172-passenger tour vessel Island Princess cruises among the Apostle Islands daily from mid-May to mid-October.

VIII.

Hiking in the Apostle Islands National Lakeshore

Hiking opportunities vary greatly from island to island. Many islands have maintained trails; while on most islands, old logging roads and trails provide some opportunities.

Stockton Island has miles of maintained trail in the vicinity or Presque Isle and Quarry Bay. On Rocky Island, approximately 3 kilometers (1 3/4 miles) of trails are located near the ranger station. Several miles have been developed on Oak Island.

Many of the old logging roads and trails are difficult to locate or follow. Hikers should use a compass and refer to a United States Geological Survey topographical map while hiking off maintained trails.

Proper equipment and preparation will help make your trip more enjoyable. Rain and cool temperatures may occur through the summer – bring appropriate clothing. Travel is often slow and difficult because of downed timber, beaver ponds, and wet areas. CAUTION: when hiking near cliffs and old quarries, loose or wet rocks may cause falls.

Insects are prevalent from May through September and can cause extreme discomfort to the unprepared. Insect repellents may be useful, but the best protection is clothing that covers exposed skin.

Backpack campers are reminded that camping permits are required. They can be obtained at the National Park Service – Bayfield, for a fee.

Fauna & Flora

The list of plants and animals living on the islands could cover numerous species from snails and aquatic life to various assortments of humans. Birds are the most visible species viewed among the islands, the greatest numbers being apparent during the spring and fall migrations. The Apostle Islands are located along many migratory flyways. This fact, combined with the relative protection birds find on the islands, makes this environment accommodating to the birds which fly over the islands as well as those which nest here. A five hour spring count of birds by the Wisconsin Ornithography Society identified 123 species on a spring day on Stockton Island in 1980. A recent study of the birds in spring has verified the casual observations of people over the past century: the number of birds and varied species is unusual. Radisson, an explorer during 1660, recorded "a good store of bustards" (swans or geese) in the Chequamegon area. The "good store of bustards" today includes hundreds of swans which can be seen during the spring and fall at the head of Chequamegon Bay. These

Many mushrooms emerge from the organic forest floors after rains.

birds, as well as many smaller species, continue to rest among the Apostle Islands on the migratory flights. Those birds which nest or have nested among the islands include gulls, loons, grebes, cormorants, herons, bitterns, ducks, geese, hawks, eagles, falcons and osprey. Of the above list, gulls, cormorants and ducks are most visible, the former often seen resting either on Lookout Point on Hermit Island or on Little Manitou. Ducks are seen along most shorelines of the islands.

Two species of gulls, the herring gull and the ring-billed gull, establish nesting rookeries on the islands. Highly populated gull nesting sites can be found along the southeast corner of Hermit Island, the north shores of Otter Island, Eagle Island and Gull Island. Smaller colonies can be found on Stockton, Raspberry, Little Manitou and Outer Islands. Another colony is strung out along the shore among the Squaw Bay Caves. It should be pointed out that all nesting sites of all birds are sensitive to human disturbance. Some sites are specifically protected, but all sites where nests are found should be avoided and left undisturbed during lengthy reproductive periods from April to August.

Terrestrial animals include snails, clams, reptiles and amphibians. Although Ireland escaped a snake population, the Apostle Islands host garter and red-bellied snakes but in no great numbers.

Mammals on the islands include members of the weasel family, fox and coyote, bear, raccoon, deer, hare, rodents and bats. None of the species are plentiful, except on some islands. Sightings of species other than rodents and beaver on Stockton and Outer Islands are a rare treat. One of the best known beaver locations is near a dam on Stockton Island where Park Naturalists leading evening hikes occasionally see or hear the animals.

White-tailed deer are at a moderate point in their population cycle on the islands. With the exception of Madeline Island where deer are often seen in fields in the mornings and evenings, few deer will be seen on the islands.

The National Park Service has this to say about the islands:
Campsites have been designated on many islands and camping is permitted only at designated sites. Camping permits are required at all sites. Permits are available from either the Little Sand Bay or the Bayfield Information Office, from the Rocky Island and Stockton Island Ranger Stations, or from any patrol ranger. Pets must be leashed or under physical control at all times.

Fires are permitted only is designated grills, pits, or rings located at each site. Trash should be discarded in receptacles (when provided) or carried back to the mainland. Do not bury refuse on the islands.

Drinking water comes from Lake Superior and from wells on some islands. Although Lake Superior's water is quite pure, it should be treated with purifying tablets or by boiling before drinking. Help others to enjoy the water by not using soap in the lake or dumping dirty wash water into the lake.

Pumping of holding tanks and bilges into the lake is a violation of State and Federal regulations and is strictly enforced by the U.S. Coast Guard, the Wisconsin Department of Natural Resources, and the National Park Service.

Swimming
Lake Superior water warms enough for swimming in shallow, protected bays. Extreme caution should be observed when swimming. NO LIFEGUARDS ARE ON DUTY within the National Lakeshore.

Warning – Dangerous Waters
Even in summer, Lake Superior's waters are dangerously cold, and sudden storms may break its surface. The temperature of the water a meter from shore may be 10°C (50°F) or less – cold enough to cause a strong swimmer to drown in 15 minutes.

The lake is large and dangerous, with a long history of violent storms and many shipwrecks. Even on seemingly calm days, boaters should keep an eye on the weather. Always, before venturing onto the lake, get the current weather forecasts from the U.S. Coast Guard Station at Bayfield, island Ranger Stations, or the marine weather frequency 162.44 MHz on your marine radio.

Administration

Apostle Islands National Lakeshore is administered by the National Park Service, U.S. Department of the Interior. A superintendent whose address is P.O. Box 721, Bayfield, WI 54814 is in immediate charge.

Please report all accidents, injuries, vandalism, and lost or found items to the nearest Ranger Station, information office, or Patrol Ranger.

Visitor Services

A Park information office in Bayfield is open daily. Interpretive exhibits and audiovisual programs are available, and Lake Survey charts and interpretive literature are on sale.

In summer, evening programs and nature walks are presented on Stockton Island and the mainland. (Check the information boards for time and locations.)

Ranger Stations on Rocky, Stockton, Devils, Outer, Michigan, Sand, and Raspberry Islands are open in summer. Rangers are in frequent radio contact with the mainland. Park patrol boats are equipped with marine radios; Rangers on patrol monitor Channel 16.

Apostle Islands National Lakeshore headquarters in Bayfield is the old Bayfield County Courthouse, a grand sandstone building from the late 1800's.

IX.

Essential Cruising and Sailing Information:

Lake Superior Navigational Charts: National Oceanic Survey, NOAA Distribution Division (C44), Riverdale, MD 20840. Chart number 14973 for the Apostle Islands. Charts of the Apostle Islands and Lake Superior are available at local marinas.

The following publications are available free from the U.S. Coast Guard, Bayfield, Wisconsin 54814:
Aids to Navigation (CG-193)
Boating Skills and Seamanship (CG)
Emergency Repairs Afloat (CG-151)
First Aid for the Boatman (AUX-206)
Federal Requirements for Recreational Boats (CG-290)

Publications from Wisconsin Department of Natural Resources, Madison, Wisconsin 53701:
Wisconsin Boating Regulations

Publications from Minnesota Department of Natural Resources, 350 Centennial Building, St. Paul, Minnesota 55155:
Boat and Water Safety
Hypothermia – The Chill that Kills

Minnesota Sea Grant Extension Program, 109 Washburn Hall, University of Minnesota, Duluth, Minnesota 55812.
Sailing on Western Lake Superior, Thomas Pollock
Superior Boating Safety, Kim Elverum

Helpful Charts, Reading, and Addresses:

Navigation Charts – U.S. Department of Commerce, NOAA, Nautical Charts, Washington, D.C., "Nautical Chart Catalog #4, U.S. Great Lakes and Adjacent Waterways."
NOAA Charts
14973 Apostle Islands
14966 Western Lake Superior
14960 Lake Superior

Brownstone and Bargeboard; A guide to Bayfield's Historic Architecture. U.W. Sea Grant Institute, 1980.

LaPointe – Village Outpost. Hamilton Ross, 1960.

The Apostle Islands – A Brief Resume of Their History. Hamilton Nelson Ross, 1973.

Chequamegon Bay and the Apostle Islands. AAUW and Marjorie Benton, 1972.

Historic Chequamegon. Rhonda Gilman, 1971.

The Bayfield Scene. Published by Bayfield Chamber of Commerce yearly.

X. Updates:

Raspberry Island – Parallel docks placed in 1987, offers greater protection from northwest seas, greater water depth than previously.

Stockton Island – Stockton has undergone several major changes: dredging, lengthening of the concrete dock and a dock perpendicular to the shore north of the main dock at Presqu'ile Bay. It creates a small harbor. Leading from the dock along the trail, you will find new interpretive centers, offering you more complete displays as well as more precise information about the islands. Rangers reside here.

The Lighthouses – For the past several years, Volunteers-in-Park have resided at the lighthouses, offering tours as well as performing protection services. The Apostle Islands lighthouses are some of the best maintained in the nation.

Long Island – This island was added to the National Lakeshore in 1987. It is designated for day-use only. Although is has beautiful beaches, there is a tangle of brush doing its best to hold back erosion, with poison ivy among them. Tread carefully. Check with the Park Service to find out current use permits.

Apostle Islands National Lakeshore Camping Policy – 1988

Camping Definitions and Regulations

Camping Permits are required for all camping within the Lakeshore.

Permits for all sites will be issued on a first come, first served basis. Permits must be obtained on the mainland, prior to departure.

Designated Sites: A signed and numbered site having, as a minimum certain fixed amenities which are a fire grill (temporary fire rings will be placed in sites without grills until new grills are received), a picnic table and a tentpad or mowed/cleared area to pitch a tent. See attached maps.

Headquarters and Little Sand Bay Rangers will check with the Dispatcher to find out what sites are available prior to filling out a permit.

Due to fragile areas on Oak Island, the campsites on the sandspit of these Islands are limited to five people per site per night.

Group Sites: A designated site which has been identified as "hard sites" and capable of withstanding heavier impact with minimal ecological damage. Amenities will include a lettered/symboled sign, one 30 inch grill, 3 picnic tables and a area to pitch tents for a maximum of 30 people. Reservations can be accepted for group sites but not before Jan. 1 of the year the group will be present. Group sites are located on Stockton Island, in Quarry Bay, Oak Island, Sand Island and Basswood Island.

Undesignated Sites: All other areas in the Park. (primarily a bushwhacking category)

Areas Closed to Camping:
1. Within view of any designated trail.
2. Within 500 feet of any designated campsite.
3. Within view of any lighthouse grounds or other historic structure.
4. Any use and occupancy tracts within the Lakeshore.
5. Devils Island, except in designated sites.
6. All of Eagle, North Twin, and Gull Islands.
7. Restricted areas are shown on the attached maps. This includes archeological sites, bird nesting areas, or other areas with fragile vegetation.
8. Within 100 feet of a flowing stream or body of water, expect in campgrounds and designated campsites.

Information from Apostle Islands National Lakeshore Handouts

The following is reprinted from Apostle Islands National Lakeshore, National Park Service, U.S. Department of the Interior publication "Diver's Guide."

Welcome SCUBA Divers

Clean, clear water, underwater rock formations, and fascinating shipwrecks offer you outstanding dives at Apostle Islands National Lakeshore.

To keep your dive safe and enjoyable, consider the following:

- Lake Superior is famous for violent weather. Monitor weather conditions and marine weather forecasts.

- Water temperatures vary with the season. Surface temperatures can reach 70 degrees F in summer, but even then divers will find under-water temperatures in the 40s and 50s. We recommend a full quarter-inch wet suit. Dry suits should be used in spring and fall.

- Visibility normally ranges from 10 to 80 feet, but can be reduced to zero under certain weather conditions. Murky runoff after storms can cloud visibility near mainland sites.

Apostle Islands National Lakeshore maintains a variety of campsites and allows back country camping on 17 of the 21 islands of the National Lakeshore.

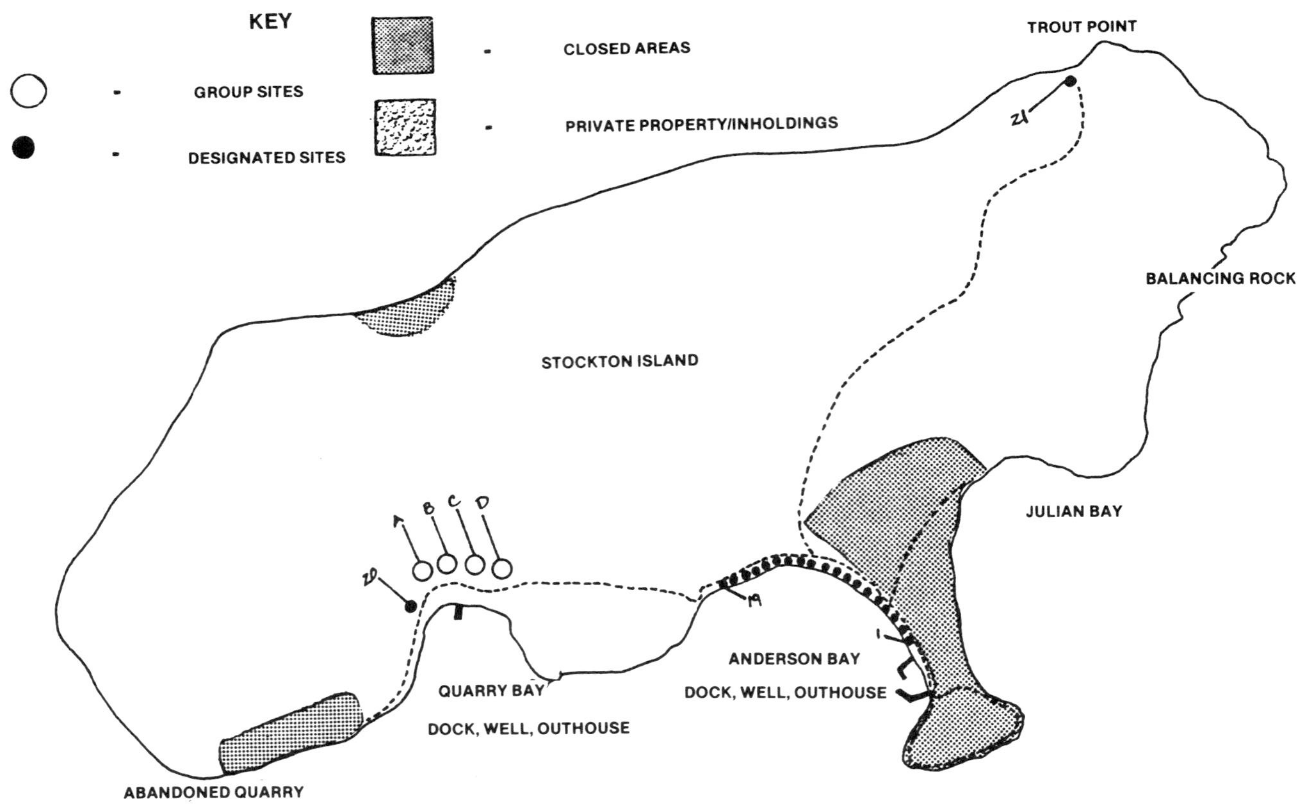
KEY
GROUP SITES
DESIGNATED SITES
CLOSED AREAS
PRIVATE PROPERTY/INHOLDINGS
TROUT POINT
21
BALANCING ROCK
STOCKTON ISLAND
JULIAN BAY
A
B
C
D
20
19
1
ANDERSON BAY
DOCK, WELL, OUTHOUSE
QUARRY BAY
DOCK, WELL, OUTHOUSE
ABANDONED QUARRY

MAINLAND

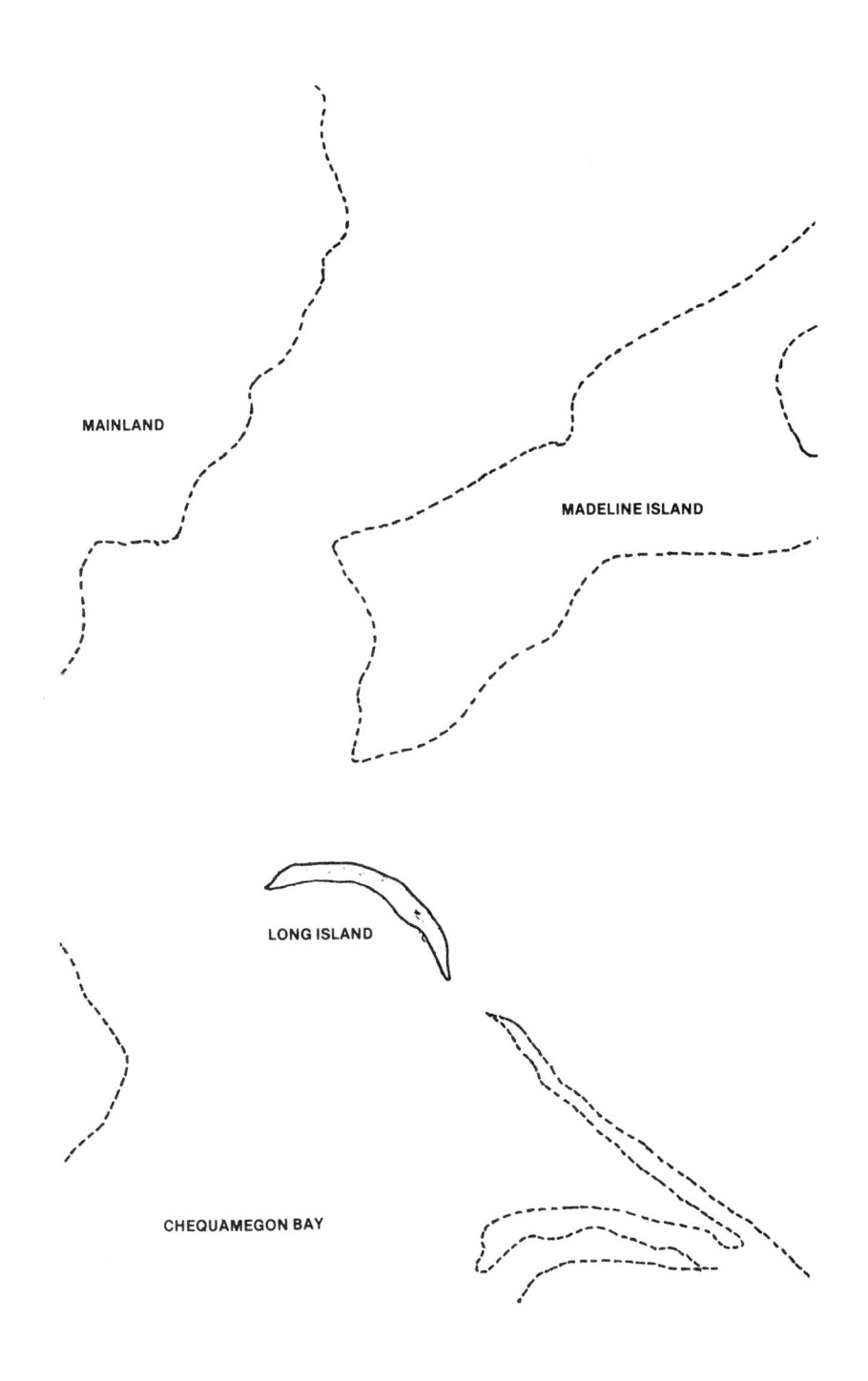

MADELINE ISLAND

LONG ISLAND

CHEQUAMEGON BAY

146

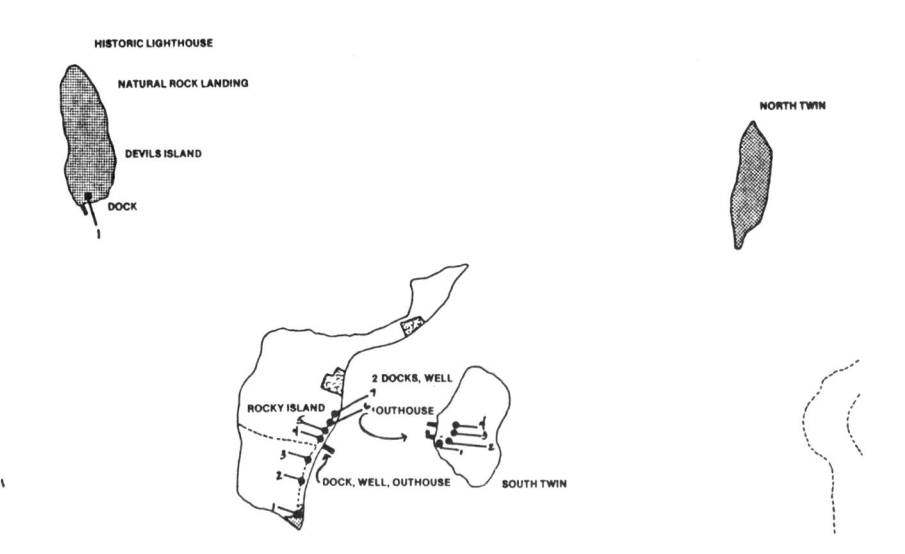

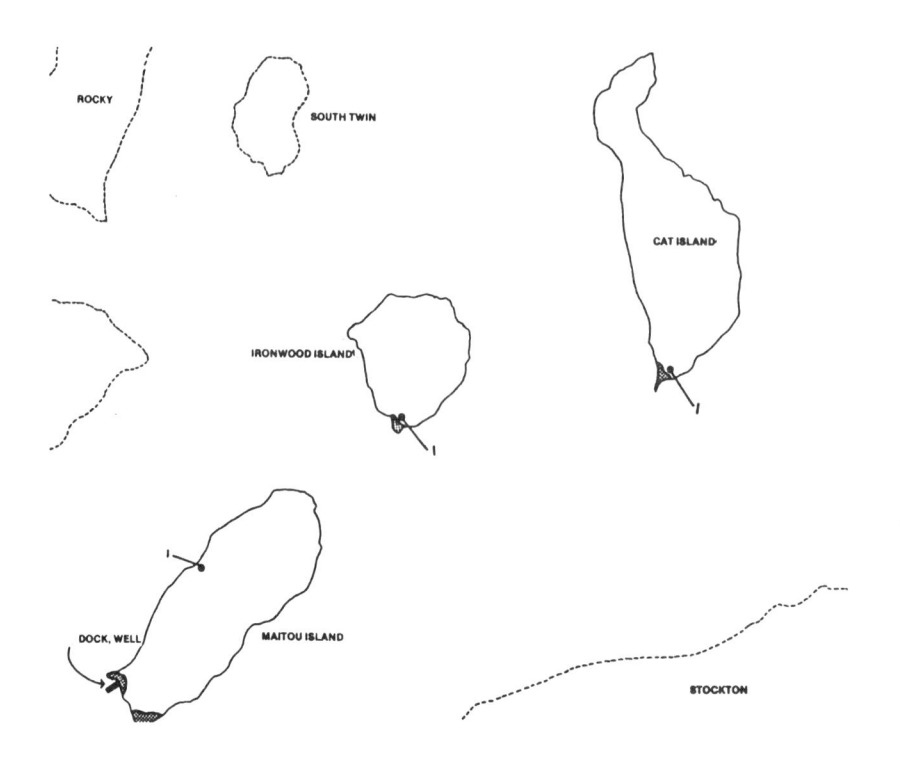

BEAR ISLAND

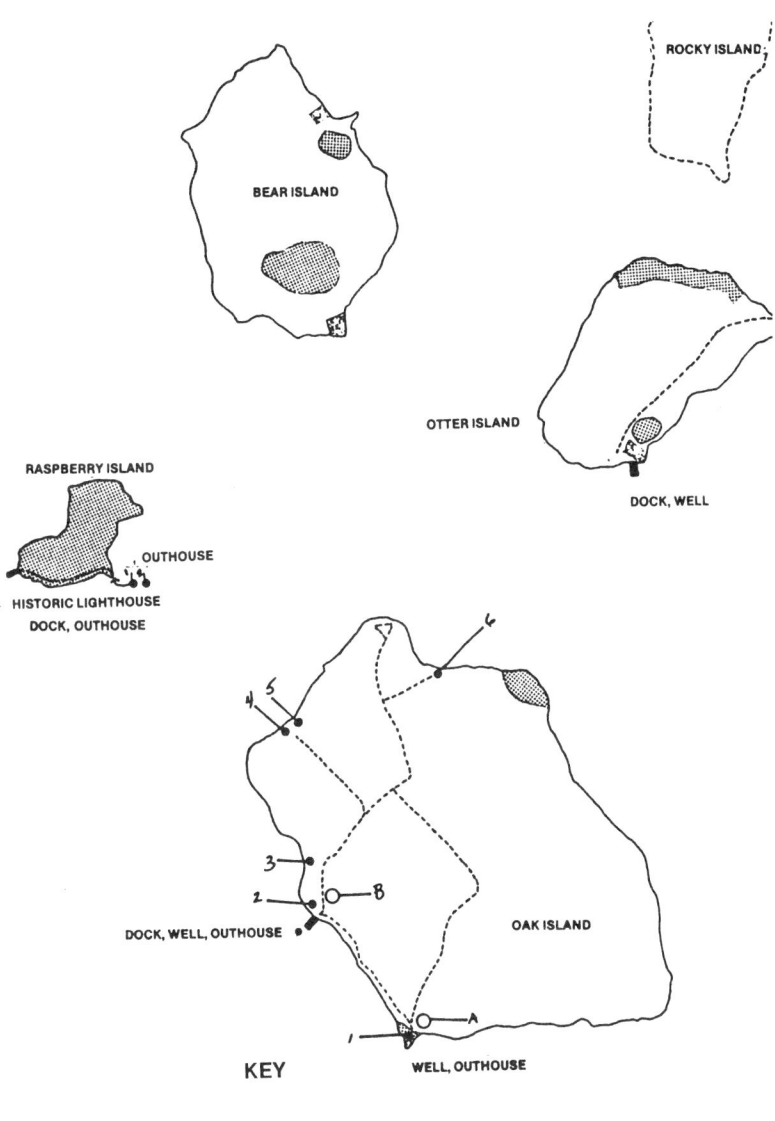

ROCKY ISLAND

OTTER ISLAND

DOCK, WELL

RASPBERRY ISLAND

OUTHOUSE

HISTORIC LIGHTHOUSE
DOCK, OUTHOUSE

OAK ISLAND

DOCK, WELL, OUTHOUSE

WELL, OUTHOUSE

KEY

○ — GROUP SITES

● — DESIGNATED SITES

▨ — CLOSED AREAS

▧ — PRIVATE PROPERTY/INHOLDINGS

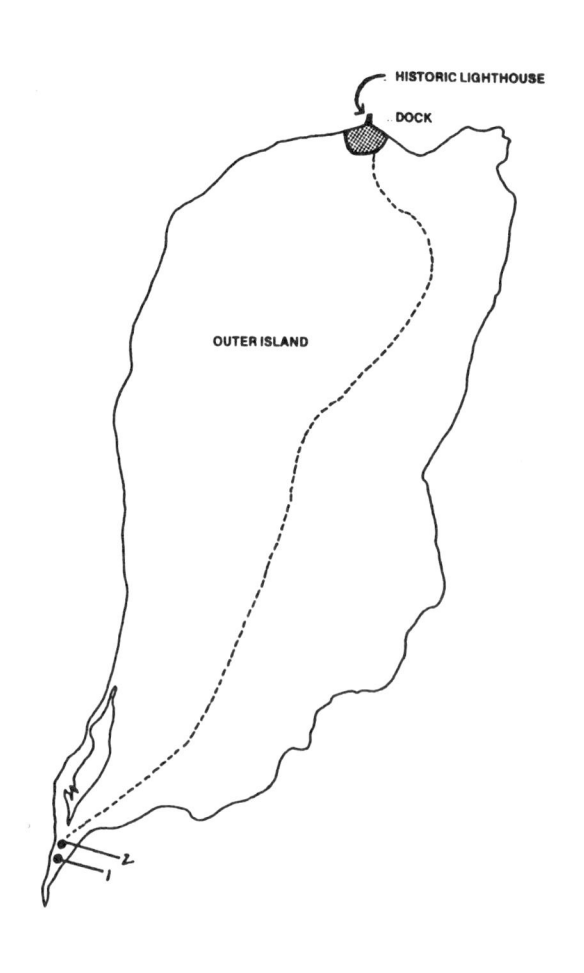

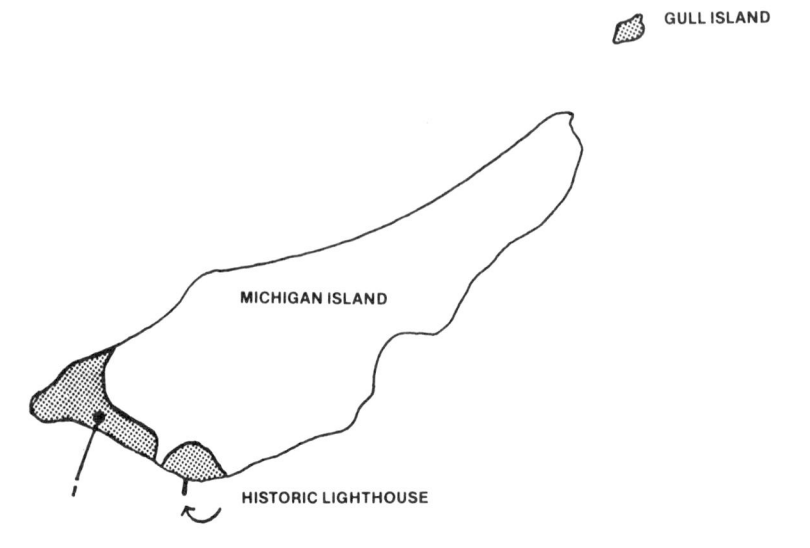

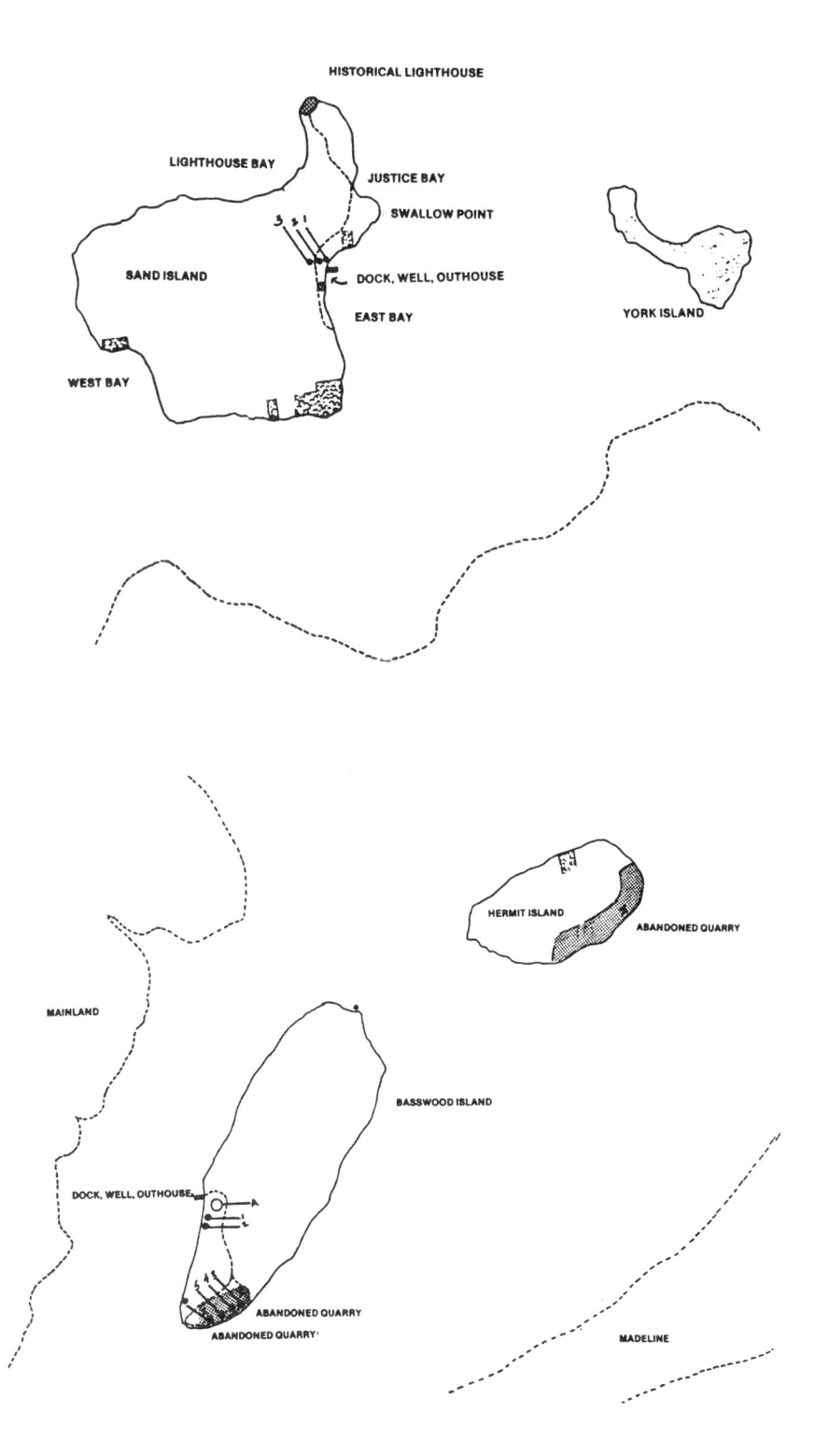

- Deep dives require specific equipment and experience. Divers not equipped or trained for depths below 130 feet should attempt such dives.

- Diving parties should know CPR and emergency procedures. Carry an adequate first-aid kit, including an oxygen delivery system.

- In an emergency, contact a park ranger. Rangers and the U.S. Coast Guard monitor marine channel 16.

- We recommend that all boaters use NOAA Charts #14973 or #14966 for navigational purposes.

Dive Sites

*-A National Park Service Diving Permit is required to dive at these sites.

Sea Caves and Cliffs

Features: Caves carved into shoreline cliffs by wave action. Visibility varies due to erosion of clay soils into the lake. Calm conditions are necessary for access.
Depths: 10 to 25 feet
Locations:
*1. Devils Island, north end. LORAN: 32341.5, 46044.5
*2. Sand Island, northeast side. LORAN: 32400.7, 46048
*3. Mainland unit, Squaw Bay, north end. LORAN: 32432, 46053
*4. Stockton Island, northeast side. LORAN: 32340, 46180

*5. "The Wall"
Features: Submerged sandstone ledges dropping into deep water.
Depth: Drops sharply to 100+ feet.
Location: Stockton Island, southwest side. LORAN: 32365.5, 46171.3

Historic Docks

Features: Submerged dock cribs near sandstone quarries active in 1890s.
Depth: 4 to 25 feet.
Locations:
*6. Basswood Island, southeast side. LORAN: 32406.7, 46176.1
*7. Stockton Island, southwest side. LORAN: 32367.8, 46170.8
*8. Hermit Island, south side. LORAN: 32381.5, 46171

151

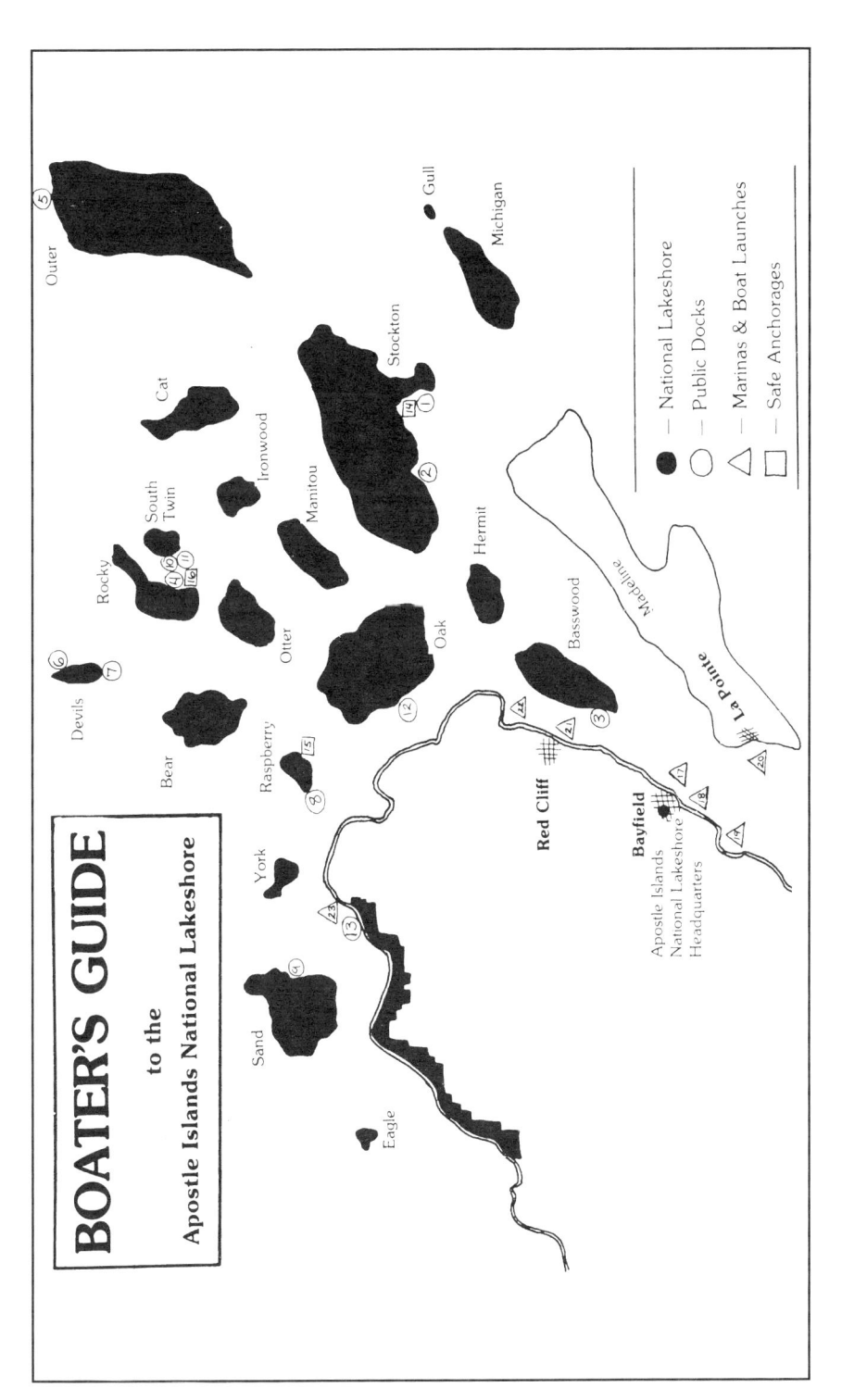

Shipwrecks

9. *Lucerne*
Schooner
Background: 195 feet long; sunk in 1886.
Features: Hull intact and upright on sand bottom. Cargo of iron ore still visible around the wreck. Visibility varies from 5 to 40 feet depending on weather. Current of about 2 knots is common.
Depth: 25 feet
Location: Long Island, northeast side, outside park boundary. LORAN: 32434.6, 46234.9

*10. *Noquebay*
Schooner Barge
Background: 205 feet lone; built 1872; burned and sunk 1905.
Features: large sections of wooden hull, scattered wreckage, boiler, and

H.D. Coffinberry, one of over 20 vessels sunk in the Apostle Islands. Coffinberry lies in Red Cliff/Schooner Bay, scuttled after burning on Basswood Island.

ship's wheel. Variably buried in sand. good visibility.
Depth: 10 to 15 feet.
Location: Stockton Island, Julian Bay. LORAN: 32351.1, 46184.5

11. *Sevona*
Bulk Freighter
Background: 373 feet long; built 1890; sunk 1905.
Features: The ship broke in half, portions of the stern's twisted steel hull and cargo of iron ore remain.
Depth: 20 to 25 feet.
Location: Sand Island shoals, outside park boundary. LORAN: 32388.1, 46032.9

12. *Pretoria*
Schooner
Background: 338 feet long; built 1900; sunk 1905.
Features: Flattened massive wooden three masted schooner-barge.
Depth: 55 feet.
Location: Northeast of Outer Island, outside park boundary. LORAN: 32288.0, 46141.1

13. *H.D. Coffinberry*
Bulk Freighter
Background: 191 feet long; built 1874; abandoned 1913.
Features: Only lower hull remains. Part of the wreck lies above water and on shore.
Depth: Partially on shore to 6 feet.
Location: Red Cliff Bay, outside park boundary. LORAN: 32395.8, 46144.7

14. *Ottawa*
Salvage Tug
Background: 151 feet long; built 1881; burned 1909.
Features: Wooden timbers and planking of lower hull.
Depth: 20 feet.
Location: Red Cliff Bay near the H.D. COFFINBERRY, outside park boundary. LORAN: 32395.8, 46144.4

15. *Fedora*
Bulk Freighter
Background: 282 feet long; built 1889; burned 1901.
Features: Lower wooden hull and steel reinforcement.
Depth: To 20 feet, partially exposed.
Location: North of Red Cliff Marina, outside park boundary. LORAN: 32403.3, 46153.5

16. *Finn McCool*
Steam Barge
Background: 135 feet long; built 1927; abandoned 1964.
Features: Relatively intact, some scattered machinery.
Depth: Up to 20 feet, partially exposed.
Location: South of Bayfield, outside park boundary. LORAN: 32423.3, 46171.5

Regulations

Diving Permits
A National Park Service Diving Permit is required within park boundaries, which includes all waters within one quarter mile of the shore. These free permits are available at park headquarters in Bayfield. Your diving registration helps us manage underwater sites.

Resource Preservation
Do not remove any artifacts. They are a unique and irreplaceable window on our own past. Exploring these treasures is not only fun and exciting, but lets us glimpse a few pages from one of the most colorful chapters in the Apostle Islands Story. Help us preserve these important sites for everyone to study and enjoy. All underwater sites and artifacts are protected by law. Possession and use of underwater metal detectors in the park is prohibited.

Dive Flag
Dive sites or boats must be marked with the standard diving flag (white diagonal stripe on a red background) or the "Alpha" flag (blue and white) whenever divers are in the water.

Anchoring
When diving on a shipwreck, avoid setting your anchor into the wreck itself.

Licensed charter dive-boat service is available in Bayfield. Lake charts #14973 and #14966, the book The Unholy Apostles – Shipwreck Tales of the Apostle Islands, and other publications are available through mail order or at the visitor center in Bayfield.

For more information contact:
Apostle Islands National Lakeshore, Route 1 Box 4, Bayfield, WI 54814; (715) 779-3397.

The following is reprinted from Apostle Islands National Lakeshore, National Park Service, U.S. Department of the Interior publication "Paddling in the Apostles."

Paddling in the Apostles

Welcome
Many people come to the Apostle Islands seeking the adventure of exploring the area by boat. Closed-cockpit craft such as sea kayaks have become very popular for travel among the islands. Operating small craft on Lake Superior is fun and exciting, but can also be hazardous. Because of the lake's power and unpredictability, the National Park Service does NOT recommend the use of small open boats or canoes for travel between islands. This guide describes conditions that may be encountered as well as preparations paddlers should make for a trip at Apostle Islands National Lakeshore. The most important prerequisite for a safe trip is good judgment. Boaters must know their equipment, know their limits, and respect the environment.

An Indian craftsman making a birch bark canoe.

Weather and Hypothermia
Lake Superior is renowned for its cold temperatures, rough seas, fog, and sudden squalls. Boaters should monitor marine weather forecasts and be constantly alert to changing conditions.

Average daytime high temperatures range from 60 degrees Fahrenheit in May, to the upper 70s in mid-summer, to the mid-60s in September. Average lows vary from 40 degrees in May, to the upper 50s in mid-summer, to 50 degrees in September. Average water temperatures in May and June are only in the 40s. Even in late summer, surface temperatures rarely exceed 60 degrees, except in protected bays. Average summer winds blow at from 5 to 20 knots with waves of from one to four feet. Winds of 30 to 40 knots and 6 to 12-foot seas are possible.

Exposure to cold temperatures, wind, and/or water can quickly lead to hypothermia. Hypothermia occurs when the body's core temperature is reduced below normal levels. If you cannot stay dry and warm under existing conditions with the clothes you have, do what is necessary to end your exposure. Watch yourself and others for uncontrollable shivering, incoherence, stumbling, and other hypothermia symptoms. If these signs are present, warm the victim immediately by giving him warm drinks and getting him into dry clothes and a warm sleeping bag.

Equipment

The National Park Service recommends that kayakers use wet suits or dry suits when paddling in the Apostles. This is especially important in spring and fall when the risk of hypothermia is high. Regulations require boaters to carry one readily accessible U.S. Coast Guard approved Personal Flotation Device (PFD) for each person on board.

Boaters should prepare for possible weather delays by packing provisions for at least one extra day. We also strongly advise boaters to pack such items as: a first aid kit, extra paddle, self-contained stove, insect repellent, compass, maps, 50 feet of lashing line, rain gear, waterproof matches, and dry storage containers.

We recommend that all boaters use Apostle Islands Lake Survey Charts #14973 or #14966. These charts and other helpful publications are available at our headquarters visitor center in Bayfield and by mail order form Apostle Islands National Lakeshore, Route 1 Box 4, Bayfield, Wisconsin 54814 (715) 779-3397.

Paddling Concerns

Sea kayaks ride low in the water and are difficult for other boaters to see. Brightly colored boats are more easily seen than those that blend with the surroundings. Bright colored clothing can also improve visibility. Some kayakers wave their paddles for visibility to approaching boats.

Sea caves are enticing but can be very hazardous in rough seas. Rebounding waves can make boat handling difficult. These shorelines offer few safe landing sites and should only be visited when conditions are calm.

It is easy to underestimate distances between destination points. Allow plenty of time to accomplish your intended route. We suggest paddling no more than 10 miles per day for beginners or 15 miles per day for seasoned paddlers. Be sure to inform a friend or relative of your travel plans so that someone will notice if you are overdue. Park rangers and the U.S. coast Guard monitor marine channel 16. Try to notify a park ranger if conditions force you to change your plans.

Camping

Visitors must obtain a permit to camp at any location in the national lakeshore. These permits are available at park visitor centers in Bayfield or at Little Sand Bay and should be obtained prior to departure for the islands. Class A campsites serve up to 7 campers and 3 tents. They are located close to docks and wells. Class B campsites are smaller and more primitive, serving up to 5 campers and 2 tents. Groups of 8 to 30 must reserve group sites on Sand, Oak, Stockton, and Basswood islands. Visitors should notify a ranger, if possible, when conditions force a change in their itinerary. Black bears inhabit several islands in the park. Campers must maintain a

Captain Ed Erickson's Memorial to Great Lakes Fishermen, designed by Harold Kar, metal artist. Windsled in background is used for winter island transportation during freeze-up and spring thaw.

clean campsite, use bearproof food storage lockers where available, or be prepared to hang food out of reach at campsites without lockers. Refer to Apostle Islands National Lakeshore's "Camping" brochure for more information.

Island Ethics

Apostle Islands National Lakeshore offers boaters the opportunity to experience and enjoy a variety of natural and cultural features. Paddlers must do their part to help protect park resources. Beaches are some of the park's most popular attractions. They also support fragile plant communities. **Camping within 100 feet of the shoreline is not permitted unless in a designated campsite.** Please walk near the water line or on established trails and take care not to trample beach grasses and lichen. Campfires are not allowed at Julian Bay beach on Stockton Island, on Raspberry Island beaches, or on any beaches adjacent to campsites with fire receptacles. Be prepared to pack out whatever you pack in. Try to leave no trace of your visit.

The following is reprinted from Apostle Islands National Lakeshore, National Park Service, U.S. Department of the Interior publication "Boater's Guide."

Boater's Guide

On The Lake

The Apostle Islands have long been a mecca for sailors and boaters. The islands' protected bays, public docks, pristine beaches, and natural beauty offer outstanding boating opportunities.

The following tips will help insure a safe, enjoyable trip.

- Obey U.S. Coast Guard inland navigation rules.
- Refer to the latest edition of NOAA Charts #14973 or #14966 for navigational purposes.
- Park rangers are equipped to help with most boating emergencies. Park rangers and U.S. Coast Guard can be contacted on marine channel 16.
- Weather conditions can change rapidly. Marine weather forecasts are broadcast on marine channels WX 1-10.
- Do not exceed your boat's carrying capacity.
- An appropriate personal flotation device (PFD) is required for each person aboard any boat.

• Do not operate a boat while under the influence of drugs or alcohol.
• Stay at least 100 feet away from flagged net buoys and/or floating plastic jugs marking the location of commercial fishing nets.
• Do not attempt to pass between the Little Manitou shoal light and Manitou Island.
• Polluting park waters is prohibited. Take trash back to the mainland.
• To protect nesting birds, boating within 500 feet of Gull and Eagle islands and the northwest shore of Otter Island is prohibited from May 15 to September 1. Do not approach within 500 feet of any active eagle nest.

At The Dock

Space is reserved at some docks for National Park Service (NPS) vessels and excursion boats. Remaining dock space is available to the public on a first come, first served basis. Please be courteous and allow as much space as possible for other boats to dock. To maximize space, Mediterranean mooring (stern or bow to the dock) is required at some docks.

For safety, the use of portable stoves or grills is not allowed on docks or on vessels tied to a dock (outside of galley areas). Swimming from docks or from vessels secured to docks is not permitted. We also ask visitors to refrain from bathing with soap directly in the lake.

LIttlw Sand Bay Hokenson historic fisheries are restored by the Park Service and tours show the lifestyle of early Norwegian settlers.

Please observe quiet hours between 10 p.m. and 6 a.m. (throughout the park). Be sure to check posted regulations upon arrival at any dock.

Anchors Aweigh

Every year, wind and waves drive anchored vessels aground on the Apostle Islands. To protect yourself and your boat...
• Always try to anchor on the lee side of an island.
• All vessels at anchor are required to exhibit anchor lights from sunset to sunrise.
• Keep a crew member on anchor watch if adverse weather threatens.
• The minimum scope of your anchor line should be seven times the distance between your boat's deck and the bottom of the lake where you are anchored.
• Set the alarm on your depth-sounder to alert you if your anchor begins to drag.
• Keep anchored vessels clear of approaches to docks and harbors.
• Be wary of shoal areas and use caution whenever beaching a boat. NPS and U.S. Coast Guard boats cannot provide towing except in emergencies.

The following is reprinted from Apostle Islands National Lakeshore, National Park Service, U.S. Department of the Interior publication "Stockton Island."

Stockton Island

This is the largest, most diverse and popular island in Apostle Islands National Lakeshore. This 10,054 acre paradise offers opportunities for hiking, camping, beachcombing, scuba diving, swimming, and bird watching. A visitor center at Presque Isle is open daily through the summer. Park rangers are available to lead walks and campfire programs and provide assistance.

Stockton Island has attracted people's interest for centuries. Archeological evidence indicates that aboriginal populations may have fished, hunted, harvested berries, and made maple syrup on the island over 1,000 years ago. By the late 1800s, Stockton Island attracted commercial interests such as fishing camps, a brownstone quarry, and lumber camps to its shores. Logging and fires changed the face of the island. Today, a new forest grows among old stumps and Stockton once again attracts people – this time for the pleasure of a near-wilderness recreational experience rather than the exploitation of its natural resources.

Sculptured Bedrock and Sand Bridges
The story of Stockton Island begins with a look at its geology. The island sits on a foundation of brownish-red sandstone called the Chequamegon Formation. About one billion years ago the sand for this formation was deposited in a type of stream called a braided river.

Like the other Apostle Islands, Stockton was shaped during the last ice age, which ended about 10,000 years ago. As continental glaciers advanced through the area, they removed everything down to the sandstone bedrock. As the glaciers retreated they left deposits of boulders, gravel, and sand called glacial till. Melt water from the glacier formed the lake we now call Superior.

In the centuries since the ice age, wind, waves, and ice have sculptured exposed shorelines into arches, caves, stacks, and cliffs. Sand eroded from these areas is deposited along more protected shores to form beaches, sandspits, and a deposit called a "tombolo".

About 5,000 years ago, Presque Isle was a small island, separated by water from its larger neighbor, Stockton Island. Shore currents carried sand southward from the larger island forming underwater sandbars that eventually contacted the smaller island. A drop in the lake level exposed this bridge of sand connecting the two islands. This sand bridge is a tombolo.

Biological Diversity
At least 429 plant species are found on Stockton Island. These are found in a variety of plant communities including northern hemlock-hardwood forest, bog, pine savanna, and dune.

Stockton's forests, wetlands, and other habitats support a variety of wildlife. Black bears, foxes, beavers, otters, and an occasional white-tailed deer are among the larger mammals found on the island. The island has one of the most concentrated populations of black bears in the world. Mice, bats, red squirrels, snowshoe hares, toads, frogs, turtles, snakes, and salamanders also make the island their home.

The island teems with diverse bird populations. Loons, mergansers, and ducks often dot the bays. Bald eagles and hawks soar overhead. Spring migration provides a symphony of warbler song in the woods. Birdwatchers also delight to find sandhill cranes and great blue herons in the tombolo lagoon.

Trails

There are about 14 miles of maintained hiking trails on the island. Off-trail travel can be strenuous. Please advise a park ranger of backcountry plans.

JULIAN BAY TRAIL, 0.4 mile

Trail booklets at the Presque Isle trailhead introduce you to the diverse plant communities along the trail. The trail ends at Julian Bay beach. (20 minutes)

ANDERSON POINT TRAIL, 1.4 miles

This trail winds through the forest along rocky shoreline between Julian Bay beach and Presque Isle dock. (50 minutes)

TOMBOLO TRAIL, 2.8 miles

Leaving the Quarry Bay trail 0.6 mile from the Presque Isle dock, this trail winds past towering pines, bogs, and along the beach, ending at the Julian Bay trail. A lagoon outlet along the beach may require hikers to make a water crossing. (2 hours)

QUARRY BAY TRAIL, 3.6 miles

This trail goes from the Presque Isle dock, through the campground, in route to Quarry Bay. (2 hours)

QUARRY TRAIL, 1.5 miles

Hike from Quarry Bay west along the shore to an abandoned quarry operated by the Ashland Brownstone Company from 1889 to 1897. (50 minutes)

TROUT POINT TRAIL, 4.7 miles

The trailhead is located on the Quarry Bay Trail 1.6 miles from Presque Isle. The path winds through Stockton's interior forest in route to the old logging camp clearing at Trout Point. ($2\frac{1}{2}$ hours)

Boating and Camping

Docks are located at Presque Isle Bay and at Quarry Bay. Docking is permitted as space is available and within posted times. Please observe all docking signs and regulations. The docks are also used by excursion and National Park Service boats.

Quarry, Presque Isle, and Julian Bays are popular locations to anchor or beach boats. Boaters should monitor marine weather forecasts, since shifting wind conditions and subsequent rough water can pose a significant threat.

A half-mile long waterfront campground is located among the pines on Presque Isle Bay. Three group campsites and one individual site are located at Quarry Bay. Another individual site is located at Trout Point. Camping permits are required and should be obtained at one of the lakeshore's mainland visitor centers. Camping reservations for groups of eight or more people can be made at lakeshore headquarters in Bayfield. For detailed information about fees and regulations, request the free publication, "Camping".

Island Ethics

We ask your help to preserve Stockton Island's beauty and ensure visitor safety. Please build campfires in fire receptacles when provided. Grilling on the dock, or on boats moored to the dock is prohibited. Campfires are not allowed at Julian Bay beach or on beaches adjacent to campsites. Burn only dead, fallen wood and do not leave fires unattended. Fireworks are not allowed.

Vegetation and soils on both sides of the tombolo are fragile and unstable. Hikers should stay on beaches or designated trails in this area. Climb bluffs only where sand ladders are provided.

Winter ice fishing among the Apostle Islands.   *Photo by Claire Duquette*

Personal flotation devices are required for each person on all vessels, including dinghies. Swimming is not allowed within 100 feet of the docks.

To lessen impacts on the island environment, do not wash dishes or yourselves directly in the lake or at the water taps. Soap and rinse where gray water can filter into the ground. Be prepared to carry all refuse back to the mainland.

Keep pets leashed and do not leave them unattended. Please observe quiet hours from 10 p.m. until 6 a.m.

Finally, do not feed bears or other wildlife. Keep your campsite clean. Campers are required to use bear-proof food storage lockers where provided. Otherwise, suspend food between two trees at least 10 feet from the ground. With your help, future visitors to Stockton will find the island as you have – in its wild and natural state.

The following is reprinted from Apostle Islands National Lakeshore, National Park Service, U.S. Department of the Interior publication "Oak Island."

Oak Island

Oak Island – land of high hills and steep valleys, sandstone cliffs and towering hardwoods. During your visit explore abandoned logging camps, breathtaking vistas, ancient beach lines, and cool, peaceful forests.

As the last glaciers receded 11,000 years ago, the ice-carved landscape that is now the Apostle Islands was slowly revealed. The waters of early Lake Superior (Glacial Lake Duluth) were so high that all the islands were submerged. Oak Island, the highest Apostle Island at 1,081 feet above sea level, was the first to emerge as lake levels lowered. Ancient beach lines, the remnants of different lake stages, can be seen in several places on the island.

During the last five thousand years, the lake level has remained relatively constant. Wind, waves, and ice have transformed Oak Island's shoreline into the terrain seen today...cliffs of glacial till, sandstone outcroppings, and sandy beaches. Most spectacular of these features are the cliffs on the north tip of the island (the highest cliffs on Wisconsin's Lake Superior shoreline) and the Hole-in-the-Wall (a sea arch along the northeast shore).

The Apostle Islands were logged in the late 1800's, the early 1900's and the 1940's through the 1950's.

Indians, Lumberjacks, and the "King"

Native people have camped and harvested food on Oak Island for centuries. Legends exist of a band of pirates using Oak Island as a look-out and base during the fur trading era of the 1700s. Land surveys conducted in the 1850s note the location of a maple "sugar bush" used by Ojibway Indians on the island.

As early as the 1850s, a cordwood business was flourishing here, supplying fuel to passing steamships. The island was subsequently logged for pine in th 1880s and 1890s, and for hemlock and hardwoods throughout the 1920s. As many as six lumber camps, including those of the Schroeder and R.D. Pike Lumber Companies, once dotted the shores of Oak Island. Some of the clearings and remnants of these camps are still evident today.

During and after the Great Depression, commercial fishermen used parts of the island as base camps. One of these men, Martin Kane, took up permanent residence near the sandspit, where he lived for over 25 years as the friendly "King of Oak Island".

Hardwoods, Deer, and Eagles

The island is covered with a mature northern hardwood-hemlock forest; including red oak, eastern hemlock, balsam fir, sugar maple, and yellow birch. Although a fire burned most of the island in 1943, many large trees survived resulting in a dense canopy and sparse understory.

A variety of mammals, birds, reptiles, and amphibians make the forest of Oak Island their home. Careful observers might discover the tracks of black bear, deer, coyote, and fox on the trails and beaches. Smaller mammals such as bats, red squirrels, mice, and voles are common. Toads and garter snakes are often seen. Loons, herring gulls, and mergansers patrol the shoreline; songbirds fill the forest with their melodies; majestic bald eagles and hawks soar overhead. Eagles frequently nest in one of the white pine trees along Oak's shoreline.

Trails

Oak Island has 11.5 miles of maintained hiking trails. Off-trail travel can be treacherous. Areas may be closed to protect nesting eagles.

LOOP TRAIL, 5.2 mi.

This horseshoe-shaped trail begins at the dock, loops north through the center of the island, then turns south to the sandspit. Walk over the highest point in the lakeshore, along ancient beach lines and past the old "sugar bush".

NORTHWEST BEACH TRAIL, 1.6 mi.

This trail leaves the loop trail 1.2 miles north of the dock and leads to a secluded beach and small group campsite.

OVERLOOK TRAIL, 1.8 mi.

Beginning 1.7 miles from the dock, this trail departs the loop trail near the highest point on the island. It leads to an overlook 200 feet above the lake with a view of ten islands and the "Hole-in-the-Wall". Stay back from the cliff edge.

NORTH BAY TRAIL, 1.1 mi.

Meander down a ravine to a campsite at the beach. This trail branches off the overlook trail 2.8 miles north of the dock.

SANDSPIT TRAIL, 1.5 mi.
Hike along the shoreline to the beach at the sandspit. Campsites, an outhouse, and an artesian well are located here. To protect the sandspit's fragile plant community, walk only on established trails or the beach.

Camping, Hunting, and Boating
Camping permits are required. The permit system allows campers to reserve campsites in advance. Reservations can be made at the Bayfield visitor center or by calling (715) 779-3397. Oak Island has four individual campsites, two large group (8-30 campers) sites, and one small group (8-10 campers) site. Camping outside of designated sites is possible, with restrictions. Campsites may be temporarily closed to prevent disturbance of nesting bald eagles.

Oak Island is a popular spot for winter camping. Ice travel is always uncertain. Stop at the Bayfield visitor center to learn about current ice conditions and obtain a camping permit. For detailed camping information, request the free brochure "Camping".

A special deer hunt for hunters using black powder rifles takes place on Oak and Basswood islands in October. A limited number of permits are available. Contact the superintendent for details.

A wooden dock is located in the middle of the west side of the island. A well and outhouse are available nearby. Maximum water depth at the end of this dock varies, but is usually about six feet. Docking is permitted as space allows.

Boaters should avoid commercial fishing nets which may be in several locations along the island's shore. Oak Island provides several possible anchorage areas, depending on prevailing wind conditions. Boaters are encouraged to monitor marine weather forecasts.

Island Ethics
Please help to preserve Oak Island's beauty and ensure visitor safety. Keep fires contained in existing fire rings or grills when provided. Burn only dead, fallen wood. Be prepared to carry all refuse back to the mainland. Use outhouses when provided; bury human waste when necessary. Do not wash dishes or yourselves directly in the lake. Soap and rinse where gray water

Apostle Islands National Lakeshore headquarters. Photo 1888, Bayfield Historical Society.

can filter into the ground. Keep pets leashed and do not leave them unattended.

Do not feed bears or other wildlife. Keep your campsite clean. Campers are required to use bear-proof food storage lockers where provided. Otherwise, suspend food and trash between trees at least ten feet off the ground.

You may discover evidence of historic logging camps. Please do not remove any artifacts or alter these sites. This deprives others of the opportunity to experience them in their original setting. Thank you for helping to preserve Oak Island's natural, scenic, and historic values.

The following is reprinted from Apostle Islands National Lakeshore, National Park Service, U.S. Department of the Interior publication "Sand Island."

Sand Island

Sand Island is the only island in Apostle Islands National Lakeshore that once had a year-round community. The community is long gone, but remnants of old structures and roads can still be found. The Sand Island Lighthouse, built in 1881 of local sandstone, stands at the northern tip of the island unaltered by more than a century of use. Sand beaches, a stand of old-growth pine trees, and the sea caves at Swallow Point are just a few of the island's spectacular natural features.

Sand and Stone

Sand Island rests on sandstone bedrock, formed from sand deposited by streams flowing over the land a billion years ago. About 10,000 years ago, glaciers stripped away layers of soil covering the sandstone, then retreated, leaving clay, sand, stones, and other material collectively known as glacial till. Lake Superior also formed in the glacier's wake. Wave action has exposed the sandstone at several places along Sand Island's shoreline. At Swallow Point, sea caves have been carved into the sandstone cliffs.

Fishermen, Farmers, and Lightkeepers

A year-round community existed on Sand Island from about 1870, when Francis Shaw built a fish camp at the southeast corner of the island, until the late 1940s. Shaw's fish camp expanded into a settlement with a farm, several houses, a rustic summer resort, and even a post office. Meanwhile, the land around East Bay was cleared and settled, primarily by immigrants from Norway. Nearly 100 fishermen and farmers were here between 1911 and 1918, when the population was at its peak. A road connected the Shaw settlement with East Bay. Children attended the island's school, open through 1928. The Sand Island Lighthouse was staffed from 1881-1920, 29 of those years by the same lightkeeper, Emmanuel Luick. Keepers and their families participated in the island's social functions, with frequent trips back and forth for mail, music, and visits with neighbors.

Today, the southeast corner of the island is still privately occupied, as are a few houses in East Bay. The West Bay Club lodge, built as a clubhouse in 1912, also remains in private hands. Please respect the privacy of these summer residents as you explore the island.

Hiking

A two-mile trail connects the campground at East Bay with the Sand Island Lighthouse. A half mile north of East Bay the trail passes through an overgrown field where hay, apples, and other crops were grown. Justice Bay, where hikers can view the Swallow point sea caves, lies at the trail's midpoint. A mile and a half north of the campground, the trail passes through an area with virgin white pines. these trees, about 240 years old, were protected within the boundaries of a lighthouse reservation. A quarter mile south of the lighthouse an overlook offers a panoramic view of Lighthouse Bay.

A second trail begins at the East Bay campground and leads west for one third of a mile to a farmsite once operated by the Noring family. The site contains some historic farm equipment and remnants of buildings. Beware of the old well located among the rubble.

Boating and Docking

There are two wooden docks for public use in East Bay. The northernmost dock is adjacent to the campground. Excursion boats also use this dock, so please observe posted restrictions. The second public dock is adjacent to the ranger quarters. A third dock to the south is privately owned. Docks at the west side and southeastern tip of the island are also private. A rock shelf near the lighthouse is fitted with mooring cleats. Extreme caution is necessary when using this landing. Underwater rocks may damage your boat, even on a calm day.

Boats often anchor at East Bay, Justice Bay, and Lighthouse Bay, depending on wind conditions. Visitors exploring the sea caves in kayaks or small boats should also note weather conditions and use caution.

Camping
Permits are required for all camping. The campground near the dock at East Bay has two class A campsites and a small group site. A group campsite is located 100 yards south of the dock. A class B campsite is located at the west end of the Lighthouse Bay beach. Wilderness camping is allowed, but camping within 100 feet of the lake is prohibited. For detailed information, request the free publication, "Camping".

A Final Note
Insects and mud can lessen your pleasure in exploring Sand Island. Long-sleeved shirts, long pants, hiking or waterproof boots, and insect repellent may help make for a more enjoyable visit. Black bears occasionally inhabit the island. Campers must take precautions to store food properly and keep campsites clean. Pack out whatever you pack in.

The days of the Sand Island community are past, but we can still glimpse reminders of that era and imagine those times. Please help us preserve the island's outstanding natural and historic resources.

The following is reprinted from Apostle Islands National Lakeshore, National Park Service, U.S. Department of the Interior publication "Basswood Island."

Basswood Island

Basswood – an island so close and yet so far. Although the Bayfield Peninsula lies just over a mile away, visitors to Basswood Island, the Ojibwa's "Wigobic Miniss", are rewarded with the isolation and solitude of an island experience.

Low cliffs of brown sandstone or banks of broken stone and red clay meet Lake Superior along Basswood's shoreline. An isolated sandstone block, called "Lone Rock" or "Honeymoon Rock" lies off the island's north tip. A dense growth of forest is broken only by several small clearings, the result of historic activities. The geology; the forests; and evidence of logging, quarrying, and farming are all vital components of Basswood's story – a story to be "read" by the observant island visitor.

Brownstone, Lumber, and Crops
The Lake Superior brownstone industry began in 1869 when sandstone from Basswood Island was selected for Milwaukee County's courthouse.

Fish tugs lay gill nets among the Apostle Islands. Gull search for an easy lunch.

Steam drills and derricks cut and moved the stone and, by 1871, brownstone was being shipped to Chicago to replace buildings lost in the great fire. In 1883, the new courthouse in Bayfield (now Park headquarters) was built of Basswood Island brownstone. Changing architectural styles and the economic crash of 1893 brought an end to the brownstone industry.

Logging on Basswood Island began in conjunction with quarry activities and continued until the 1950s. Eastern hemlock, one of the first species harvested, was important to the leather industry. Two million board feet of white pine were harvested from the island's northeast side in the 1890s. In the 1940s, a small logging camp was located in what is now a campground near Basswood Island's dock. This operation harvested aspen and fir for pulpwood and yellow birch for veneer.

Several farmers have taken advantage of the island's extended growing season. The McCloud-Brigham farm, located in the north central portion of the island, was the largest. The McClouds produced corn, tomatoes, and squash for workers at the quarry in the early 1870s. In later years, the Brighams planted an orchard of apples and plums and brought cows to the farm. None of the five buildings once at the site remain standing.

Flora and Fauna
Basswood Island is cloaked in a northern hardwood/hemlock forest of red oak, sugar maple, quaking aspen, white and yellow birch, eastern hemlock, balsam fir, white cedar, red, and white pine. A few basswood trees are also present.

Because of the dense forest canopy, most flowers bloom in spring before the trees leaf out. Starflower, clintonia, Canada dogwood, rose twisted stalk, and dwarf ginseng are a few of the early varieties.

Basswood Island is home for a variety of wildlife. Beavers and otters visit the pond in the abandoned quarry. Red squirrels are common. This island also supports a small population of white-tailed deer. A variety of habitats attract many of the 100+ birds species that nest in the Apostle Islands, including bald eagles. Special closures may be enacted to protect young eagles during the nesting season.

Much of Basswood Island is low and remains wet through spring into early summer, providing ideal conditions for mosquitos. Protective clothing and insect repellent are musts if one hopes to enjoy the sights of Basswood Island during this season.

Trails

A $5\frac{1}{2}$ mile loop trail begins and ends in a clearing up the hill from the dock. This trail proceeds northeast across a ravine, then $1\frac{3}{4}$ miles to the McCloud-Brigham farm site. From there the trail follows an old logging road to the east side of the island, then swings south for $2\frac{1}{4}$ miles to some excellent overlooks of the main quarry area. Several large blocks of cut brownstone lie in the quarry opening and rusted parts of old equipment can still be found. From the quarry, the loop trail turns north for $1\frac{1}{2}$ miles through the forest to the dock clearing.

Boating, Camping, and Hunting

A 70 foot long dock is located midway up the west side of the island near the outlet of a small stream. The maximum depth of water at the end of the dock is 4-6 feet. Boaters planning to moor overnight are cautioned that this dock is exposed to winds from the southwest and northwest. Captains are encouraged to monitor marine weather forecasts for weather and wave conditions.

Basswood's proximity to mainland harbors at Bayfield, Red Cliff, and Schooner Bay make it one of the most accessible islands. Persons traveling to the island in small boats, canoes or kayaks should pay attention to weather conditions and proceed with caution.

Permits are required for all camping and are available at the national lakeshore visitor center in Bayfield. Four campsites are located at the south end of the island near the brownstone quarry. Two more campsites are located near a clearing 200 yards from the dock. A large group campsite is in the clearing, along with a vault toilet and a well. For detailed camping information, request the free publication, "Camping".

A special deer hunt for hunters using black powder rifles takes place on Oak and Basswood islands in October. A limited number of permits are available. Contact the superintendent for details. Visitors to the island in October should exercise caution by wearing high visibility clothing, keeping on established trails, and using designated campsites.

Island Ethics

Please help to preserve Basswood Island's beauty and ensure visitor safety. Keep fires in existing fire rings or grills when provided. Burn only dead, fallen wood. Be prepared to carry all refuse back to the mainland. Use pit toilets when provided; bury human waste when necessary. Do not feed bears or other wildlife. Keep your campsite clean and hang food between trees at least 10 feet off the ground. Pets must be leashed and constantly attended.

Devils Island tower overlooks 30'-50' sandstone cliffs.

Please do not remove any artifacts from the island's historic sites. this is not only illegal, but deprives other visitors of the opportunity to experience them in their original setting. Thank you for helping to preserve Basswood Island's natural, scenic and historic values.

The following is reprinted from Apostle Islands National Lakeshore, National Park Service, U.S. Department of the Interior publication "Sea Caves."

Sea Caves

Centuries of wave action, freezing, and thawing have sculpted shorelines throughout Apostle Islands National Lakeshore. Some of the Great Lakes' most spectacular scenery occurs where nature has carved intricate caves into sandstone of the Devils Island Formation. Delicate arches, vaulted chambers, and hidden passageways honeycomb cliffs on the north shore of Devils Island, Swallow Point on Sand Island, and northeast of Cornucopia on the mainland. Visitors are drawn to Apostle Islands National Lakeshore in summer and winter to visit the sea caves and witness Lake Superior's ever-changing handiwork.

Geology
The story of the Devils Island Formation begins over one billion years ago. At that time, rivers and streams carried sandy sediments from hills in what is now southern Minnesota to a basin where the Apostle Islands are now found. These rivers, known as braided streams, carried sediment that slowly filled the basin, forming a sand flat. When that occurred, this area was covered with many shallow ponds, some only a few inches deep, connected by shallow channels. Sand deposits in this environment were thinly-bedded, fine-grained, and extensively ripple marked. these deposits became the sandstone known as the Devils Island Formation.

Where wave action erodes and undercuts the base of a cliff, a feature known as a reentrant develops. Sea caves are produced when a number of reentrants join behind the face of a cliff. leaving behind supporting pillars and arches. They develop most easily where the sand layers comprising a rock formation are very thin. Cliffs carved from exposures of the Devils Island Formation at Devils Island, Sand Island, and on the mainland feature thin layers of sandstone. this easily eroded formation is the primary source of Apostle Islands National Lakeshore's spectacular array of sea caves.

Through the Seasons
The beauty of the caves varies dramatically with the season. In February, an ice bridge might connect Sand Island to the mainland. The lake near the mainland sea caves is usually a frozen white expanse. Lakeshore cliffs form a crimson border to this arctic landscape. Pillars of ice extend to the cliff tops where waterfalls have hardened in place. Frozen lakewater encrusts the base of the cliffs. Inside the caves is a fairyland of needle-like icicles. The formations change from chamber to chamber and from day to day.

In summer, the variegated red sandstone is sandwiched between sapphire lake and emerald forests. Large waves generate plumes of spray and thunderous explosions as they surge into the sea caves. While visitors must enjoy these scenes from a distance, such is not the case when the lake is tranquil. Under calm conditions, kayakers can explore the caves' deepest recesses while listening to the murmur of water against rock.

Getting There
In summer, the sea caves are best seen by boat. The Apostle Islands Cruise Service offers daily trips past the Devils Island sea caves from late May through the middle of October. On Wednesday and Saturday evenings in July and August, the concessioner also offers a sunset cruise to the mainland sea caves. Kayak outfitters in Bayfield guide day trips to the mainland sea caves throughout the summer. Kayakers with their own boats wishing to visit the mainland sea caves will find a good launch point at the end of Meyers Road near the Meyers Beach picnic area. Meyers Road is located about 18 miles west of Bayfield off Highway 13. Boaters wishing to visit the Sand Island caves will find a boat launch at Little Sand Bay, 13 miles north of Bayfield. The Swallow Point sea caves on the east side of Sand Island are about four miles from Little Sand Bay. The Devils Island sea caves are 14 miles from Little Sand Bay or 22 miles from Bayfield.

To reach the mainland sea caves in winter, visitors should drive to the end of Meyers Road and park at the Meyers Beach picnic area. The bay near Meyers Road is frequently covered with ice for some or all of the period from late January to mid-March. If the bay is sufficiently frozen, visitors can walk, snowshoe, or ski northeast across the ice to the cliffs. The caves begin about one mile from Meyers Beach.

Safety
Visitors to the caves face a number of potential hazards. Boaters should avoid sea caves when conditions are rough. Get the marine weather fore-

cast before leaving on your trip. Personal flotation devices should be worn. Kayakers should not visit the caves alone. When walking along cliff tops remember that this is an eroding shoreline. Stay back from the edge.

Winter visitors need to be especially careful. Warm clothing is a must. Sub-zero temperatures and bitter wind-chills are common. Walking on ice can be extremely dangerous and demands caution: when in doubt, don't go out. If you go, watch for newly formed cracks or soft spots in the ice, wear sturdy boots to prevent slipping, and watch for any signs of falling ice near the caves. Mainland visitors near Meyers Road can receive information on ice conditions at the mainland caves by tuning their radio to AM 1610. People planning a winter trip to the mainland sea caves can still call the Apostle Islands Ice Line at (715) 779-7007 for current information about ice conditions. For general information and up-to-date weather conditions call (715) 779-3397. Ice conditions can change rapidly, so keep safety in mind at all times.